KITTATINNY TRAILS

KITTATINNY TRAILS

Robert L. Boysen

NEW YORK-NEW JERSEY TRAIL CONFERENCE

Library of Congress Cataloging-in-Publication Data

Boysen, Robert L., 1940-
Kittatinny trails / Robert L. Boysen.-- 1st ed.
p. cm.
Includes bibliographical references.
ISBN 1-880775-38-7 (alk. paper)
1. Hiking--Kittatinny Mountain Region--Guidebooks. 2. Trails--Kittatinny
Mountain Region--Guidebooks. 3. Kittatinny Mountain Region--Guidebooks. I.
New York-New Jersey Trail Conference. II. Title.
GV199.42.K55B69 2004
917.49'76--dc22
2004019302

Cover photo:
Tillman's Cascade, one of several waterfalls seen from the Tillman's Ravine Trail in Stokes State Forest.

Dedicated to

GAY LORRAINE BURGIEL
1939-2004

Dear and Faithful Friend

TABLE OF CONTENTS

*DWGNRA: Delaware Water Gap National Recreational Area   SSF: Stokes State Forest
WSF: Worthington State Forest   HPSP: High Point State Park*

Acknowledgments

This guide could never have been written without the help of many, many people. I have tried to list the most significant contributions below. My heartfelt thanks to all who have helped, and I sincerely hope I have not underestimated anyone's contribution.

Rose Marie Boysen	Typing the text, company on the trails, GPS data gathering and moral support (she feeds and clothes me as well)
Gay L. Burgiel	Copy editing, company on the trails, GPS data gathering
Jim Canfield	Extensive GPS data contributions
John Grob	Company on the trails, GPS data contributions
Laura Newgard	Trail information
David Day	Trail information

Park Managers	Information on park rules and facilities.
	    -Ernie Kabert, Worthington State Forest
	    -Paul Stern, Stokes State Forest
	    - John Keator, High Point State Park
	    -Brad Clawson, DWGNRA

George Petty and the Publications Committee	Advice and counsel on map design, elevation profiles, trail descriptions
Nora Porter	Book design
Sandy Parr	Trail information and geology education
Larry Wheelock	Trail and park information
Hercules Hound	Hiking companion extraordinaire

Disclaimers

About 140 miles of trails are covered by this guide, 45 of them part of the Appalachian Trail (AT). All but about ten miles of the AT and about five miles of the non-AT trails have been hiked by the author during the past few years. Essentially all of the mapping data is from hand held GPS or from aerial photography in the form of USGS quadrangle maps. The elevation profile data is from USGS maps as well.

The emphasis is on the day hiker. There are several AT through hiker guides, so there was no need to duplicate these. The AT in this book is divided into ten sections which are described and mapped with the adjacent non-AT trails.

Change to trail descriptions is to be expected. Natural forces, trail crews, trail maintainers, and park administrations all produce changes for their good reasons. The information contained in the guide cannot be taken as permanently and absolutely correct. An accurate and thorough description unchangeable with time is an impossibility. The New York-New Jersey Trail Conference (NYNJTC) tries to keep its trail guides up to date by publishing revisions at regular intervals. We encourage hikers to submit information on trail changes to our website at www.nynjtc.org, or by contacting our office at 201-512-9348.

Like other active sports, hiking can be hazardous. It is not the purpose of this guide to provide trailside medical advice. All hazards cannot be effectively communicated. No safety advice by this guide is intended, since the author is certainly not a safety expert. We urge readers to carry appropriate first aid equipment, to resist attempting hikes beyond their capabilities, and to avoid taking unnecessary risks in the woods. Information on hiking safety can be found in *Health Hints for Hikers* published by the NYNJTC, or other similar publications.

—*Robert L. Boysen*

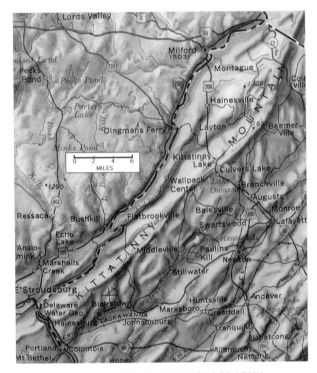

KITTATINNY RANGE TOPOGRAPHY

INTRODUCTION

Description of the Kittatinny Range

The Kittatinny Range is the New Jersey section of a very long Appalachian Mountain ridge line which extends almost continuously from Virginia to New York with only a few short breaks. The name is descriptive; Kittatinny means "endless mountain" in the Lenni Lenape language. One of the breaks in the endless mountain is the Delaware Water Gap (DWG). The Delaware River, which forms the boundary between New Jersey and Pennsylvania, flows through the Gap.

In New York the name given to this ridge line is the Shawangunks, and in eastern Pennsylvania it is known as the Blue Mountains. In West Virginia and Virginia it is usually known as the North Mountain.

The ridge forms the northwestern edge of the Great Valley of the Appalachians, which also runs continuously from the Hudson River to southern Virginia and is the dividing line between the more ancient mountains of the Appalachian Highlands/Blue Ridge Ranges and the relatively younger mountains of the Kittatinny/Shawangunk/Blue Mountain/North Mountain ridge line.

The topographic map on the previous page illustrates this geography. It is essentially a single major ridge line with several gaps and with a few parallel smaller ridges on both sides of the main ridge.

In New Jersey most of the Kittatinny Ridge is preserved as public land.

Two state forests, a state park and a National Recreation Area cover virtually the entire ridge. They are*

Delaware Water Gap National Recreation Area (DWGNRA)	
in New Jersey	47.3 sq. miles
in Pennsylvania at the DWG	9.2 sq. miles
Worthington State Forest	12.1 sq. miles
Stokes State Forest	22.2 sq. miles
High Point State Park	24.2 sq. miles

In these preserves 115 square miles of beautiful country have been set aside for public recreation within easy access of millions of urban and suburban people. This is rather amazing considering that New Jersey is more densely populated than any other state in the Union and almost every nation on earth**. About one of every four Americans lives within a two-hour drive of the Kittatinnies.

Based on these statistics one might expect heavy use and overcrowding of trails, but this is not really the case.

The shaded part of the location map on the following page includes these four parks and is the area covered by this guide.

Brief History

The earliest known human habitation of the area is thought to be about 8000 B.C.E. Only scant archeological evidence exists between that time and the first contact with Europeans in the 17th century, which marks the beginning of the historic era. The tribe then occupying the Kittatinnies was the Minsi branch of the Lenni Lanape or "Delaware" Amerindians, one of the group of tribes speaking the Algonquin language. The Delaware River Valley and nearby ridges between the Delaware Water Gap and Port Jervis are often known as the "Minisink" area in reference to the Minsi tribe.

The Minsis obtained food from agriculture, hunting, and gathering. They lived in wigwams and settlements were not fortified, indicating a rather secure existence. Several Minsi archeological sites exist in the area.

---

*Estimated areas.
**Exceeded only by the Netherlands, South Korea, Taiwan and Bangladesh.

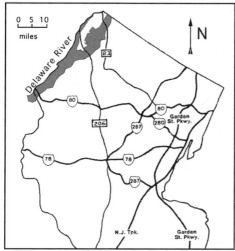

Northern New Jersey and the Kittatinny Range

The first significant European contact occurred at about 1650, and most of the Minsi had left the area just a hundred years later, although the number of European settlers was not very great at that time.

The last known Amerindian raid on European settlements in New Jersey occurred in 1776 during the American Revolution at Montague, where US Route 206 today crosses the Old Mine Road and the Delaware River. This raid was almost certainly led by Iroquois, who were allies of the British during the Revolutionary War, but probably included many Minsi. The ire of the Minsi had been raised by the "walking purchase" of 1737, when the Pennsylvania colony used a treaty technicality to vastly expand the area of purchase to include basically all of the Minisink on the Pennsylvania side of the river.

One of the great tragedies of Amerindian history is that they chose the losing side during the American Revolution. It colored American attitudes toward Amerindians for many decades to come.

Continental troops under General Sullivan totally devastated the Iroquois homeland in the Finger Lakes region of New York in 1779, two years before the British surrender at Yorktown. There were no more raids.

European exploitation of the Minisink occurred very early compared with other locations in northwestern New Jersey. The Dutch, who had established New Amsterdam (New York) in 1637, rapidly extended their settlements up the Hudson River Valley. They settled Kingston, New York (then called Esopus), in 1652. Travelling the valleys of the Appalachians southwest from Kingston, one eventually ends up in Port Jervis, and then, following the

Delaware, at the Delaware Water Gap. Someone discovered in the mid-17th century that high grade copper ores were easily accessible on the New Jersey side of the Minisink. By 1656 the Dutch were mining copper ore just north of the Delaware Water Gap. They built the Old Mine Road extending more than 100 miles to Kingston to transport the ore to the navigable Hudson and eventually to Holland itself. Brass, of which copper is a major component, was a militarily strategic metal in the 17th century. The remains of their mines are visible today just off the Coppermines Trail. The enterprise did not last long, however. The English took over the entire Dutch colony in 1664.

Agricultural settlement of the Minisink, mostly by Dutch, occurred much later, starting about 1700. European occupation of the neighboring Great Valley in New Jersey, on the other hand, occurred in about 1740 and included mostly Germans and British.

The area remained chiefly agricultural for over 100 years, gradually increasing in population to a saturation level about 1850.

In 1829 the first resort hotel, the Kittatinny House, was built just north of the Delaware Water Gap. The resort industry grew during the 19th century, eventually including 50 hotels. This phase peaked just after the beginning of the 20th century, after which a slow decline in population occurred. Agricultural competition from the opening of the Great Plains made farming in the mountainous and stony Kittatinny area less viable. And advances in transportation technology (chiefly the railroad) created other resort opportunities for the people of the northeastern United States.

In 1962 the U.S. Congress authorized a project to establish a dam on the Delaware River at Tocks Island, about three miles north of the Delaware Water Gap, which would create an eight-mile-long reservoir. The purposes of the project were flood control, water storage, and hydroelectric energy production. The opposition began almost immediately, but so did the preparations.

By the time the project was finally abandoned in 1974, the federal government had acquired most of the land to be covered by the reservoir. They had also destroyed much of the housing in the purchase area. After the decision to convert the land to the Delaware Water Gap National Recreation Area (DWGNRA), they continued to pull down housing, provided it had little or no historic interest. Most of the existing farmland was abandoned, so there are many acres of former farm fields in the DWGNRA now in various stages of reforestation. Reforestation occurs rather quickly in New Jersey. Within 20 years the new growth has progressed enough so that it is irreversible without major effort. Within 100 years most casual observers would regard a former field as simply another woodland. A few fields have been preserved by leasing them to local farmers living outside the National Recreation Area.

This portion of the Minisink is slowly returning to its former wild state. While many see this as a positive development, people who knew and loved the land the way it was decry the destruction of beautiful and viable farmsteads and farming communities. In addition many historic structures have been or are being abandoned or destroyed, although some effort is being made to maintain the most significant, especially in the Millbrook and Walpack Center villages.

The state forests and High Point State Park (HPSP) have existed a lot longer than the DWGNRA. Parts of Stokes State Forest (SSF) were the first lands purchased for public use by the State of New Jersey. During the 1930s, SSF was the site of Civilian Conservation Corps (CCC) camps. The CCC constructed Sunrise Mountain Road, built the Sunrise Mountain shelter and developed the Ocquittunk and Shotwell campgrounds. CCC teams were major contributors to building the 24 trails of SSF. Most of the pine and or spruce plantations scattered throughout the forest were planted by the CCC.

High Point State Park has been used for recreation for over 150 years. As early as 1855, the public began using the area informally for picnics and outings. The High Point Inn, a large resort facility, was built in 1890, but it lasted less than 20 years as an inn. John F. Dryden purchased most of the lands in 1911. He intended to use it as a private nature preserve, but he died soon after the purchase and the property devolved to his son-in-law, Anthony Kuser. In 1923 the Kuser family donated the property to the state. Soon after they acquired the land the state hired the Olmsted brothers to design a development plan. Many of the park's current features were built over the next 20 years based on that plan.

In the 1930s the CCC was also active at HPSP, developing the Lake Marcia and Saw Mill Pond areas, as well as extending the trail network.

Worthington State Forest (WSF) contains some of the most rugged terrain in New Jersey. It was initially preserved as a private deer park for industrialist C.C. Worthington. The state leased the tract as a game preserve in 1910, and finally purchased it in 1954.

Flora and Fauna

The entire Kittatinny Ridge is covered with mixed hardwood (broadleaf) and northern conifer forest. In general, the hardwoods dominate.

The most common large hardwoods are oaks, hickories, birches, beeches, walnuts, maples and poplars. Each of these is a family of species. Overall there are 50 to 100 large tree species present on the Kittatinny Ridge.

The most common conifers are hemlock and red cedar which can locally predominate, hemlocks in damp ravines, cedars in overgrown fields. Spruce and pine are less common, and often have been planted where they appear.

Smaller trees, shrubs and ground plants are equally prolific, the number and type too many to mention here. There are also many domesticated and non-native plant species at all levels because the area was once intensively agricultural and well populated.

The type, sizes and density of vegetation vary greatly over time in overgrown fields. The sequence of dominance is usually ground plants, shrubs, small

Small herd of whitetail deer

trees, red cedars, large young trees in dense stands, and finally large mature trees in less dense stands with little or no underbrush.

Mature forest is the most easily negotiated on foot. At some stages overgrown fields can be essentially impenetrable.

Wildflowers are common, especially in areas free of trees. They can be seen any time during the growing season from April to October.

Many medium- to large-size animal and bird species have learned to thrive close to human kind. Contrary to the popular image, New Jersey is a prime area for wildlife viewing. The number of interesting species is matched in very few places on earth. A hospitable well-watered natural environment and a human population which is not inclined to eat everything that moves, and which, in fact, provides lots of food from grain fields, bird feeders, and garbage cans, lead to this unusual phenomenon.

As a case in point, I have listed below the larger animal and bird species I have personally spotted in the last 12 months (and I probably forgot several).

Common Animals and Birds
(defined as those spotted by the author in the past 12 months)

Common Animals	*Common Birds*
white tailed deer	black duck
beaver	blue heron
black bear	Canada goose
cottontail rabbit	crow
coyote	great egret
gray squirrel	great horned owl
red squirrel	grouse
groundhog (eastern marmot)	pheasant
mink	flicker
opossum	pileated woodpecker
raccoon	red-tailed hawk
red fox	ruby throated hummingbird
skunk (smelled, not spotted)	turkey vulture
turtles (various)	swan

frogs (various)
brown bat
snakes (various)

songbirds, various including:
  cardinal
  eastern bluebird
  barn swallow
  goldfinch
  yellow warbler

New Jersey is also a game hunter's paradise, the biggest challenge perhaps being able to find a place far enough from the nearest house to allow for safe firearms discharge. Refer to the reference section for a list of hunting seasons and areas.

The Seasons

The weather in the Kittatinnies is very seasonal and very variable. Average high temperatures range from the mid 30s (Fahrenheit) in January to the mid-80s in July. Deviations from average of up to 15ºF are common. So, in July, almost all the time, the daily high temperature will be between 70ºF and 100ºF, and in January, between 20ºF and 50ºF.

The daily average low temperature is 15ºF to 20ºF lower than the average high.

Precipitation is also highly variable, averaging about 3.7 inches per month, but commonly varying from one inch to eight inches in a month. Fall is a bit dryer on average than the rest of the year.

Snowfall average yearly total is about 36 inches. Snow can fall anytime between late November and early April. The ground is snow covered, on average, for about six weeks during the year. This can easily vary from two weeks to ten weeks. Depth of snow is rarely above two feet and often just two to three inches.

Although the maximum elevation range from valley to peak is only about 1500 feet, there is some variation in weather conditions with elevation. The higher ridges will be somewhat cooler in all seasons and snowfall there is likely to be greater.

Winds come mostly from the northwest. Wind speeds seldom exceed 25 mph and usually are in the five to ten mph range.

The hardwoods lose their leaves between October 10 and November 10, giving an astounding display of color during that period. The height of color is usually around October 20.

After the loss of leaves, many winter views open up which are merely walls of green during leaf season. In mid-April to mid-May the new crop of leaves appears and the winter views disappear again.

Canada goose

Hiking can be done in any season. Humid heat and prolific insects often make hiking in mid-summer less desirable, and in mid-winter snowshoes or skis may be needed if snow cover is over six inches. The prime hiking seasons are spring and fall.

Snow shoeing and cross-country skiing are usually possible on the trails for some period of time each winter. Both are permitted on all trails except the Appalachian Trail (AT), which permits snow shoeing only. A cross-country ski concession is run from High Point State Park (HPSP) each winter. Several trails are machine maintained and rental equipment and refreshments are available at a small lodge. Some trails in HPSP are also reserved for snowmobiles and dog sleds when appropriate. Refer to the reference section for more details.

A trail maintainer at work

GUIDE TO THE
GUIDE

The Kittatinny Range, the region covered by this guide, is 40 miles long and on average only about three miles wide. Trailheads at the northeastern end are 50 or 60 road miles from trailheads at the southwestern end. The range runs almost exactly northeast to southwest with a slight tilt to the north-south direction.

The AT is the "unifying" trail in the area, running the full length of the ridge from southwest to northeast. This guide covers an additional 59 trails, some of which connect to the AT, some of which do not.

The trails are divided into 13 regions to facilitate understanding of the geography and to group together trails which can generally be reached from a single public road by the day hiker. Because the guide is written with the day hiker in mind, and not the AT through hiker, the description of the AT is divided into ten sections, and each section is described in the most appropriate of the 13 regions. Although there are many other guides for AT through hikers, the AT is described here for the day hiker. See the reference section for other guides to the AT.

Each trail description includes information on trail access, trail surface, scenery and points of interest, and amount of climbing. In addition the trails and AT sections are illustrated with detailed maps and elevation profiles. The map and profile data are all derived, with few exceptions, from recent mapping (2002 to 2003) by hand-held GPS devices or from USGS aerial photography. The maps include latitude and longitude tick marks for use by hikers with hand-held GPS equipment. A grid can be drawn, if desired, simply by ruling straight lines between tick marks. The map datum used is WGS 84, so if the user is comparing maps in this guide with USGS maps, some (usually small) deviations may be noted, since USGS uses a NAD 27 map datum standard.

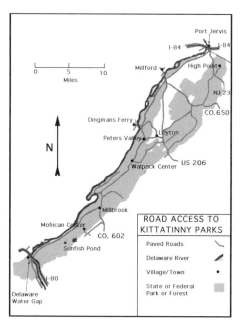

MAPS AND ELEVATION PROFILES

An overall area map showing key public road access to the area is presented above. Despite their proximity to the most populous region in the USA, road access to Kittatinny trails is fairly limited. In the 40-mile length of the area, only four bridges cross the Delaware River and two of them are at the extreme ends of the region; i.e., in the 40 miles between I-84 and I-80, only two bridges cross the Delaware River.

Similarly, only four public roads cross the 40-mile stretch of the Kittatinny range: County Route 602, US Route 206, Deckertown Turnpike and State Route 23.

The map below delineates the 13 regions used in the guide, along with public access roads for each region.

A miniature replica of the area map appears at the beginning of each section and the general location of each section is shown on each miniature.

The symbols used on the trail maps and elevation profiles are generally

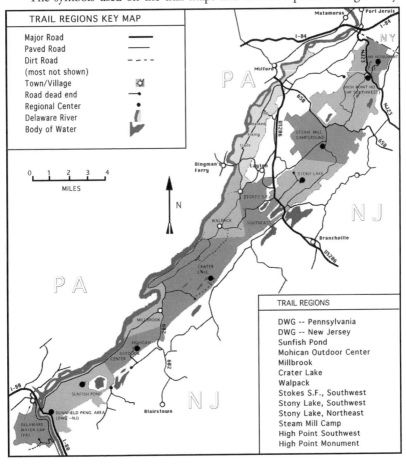

TRAIL REGIONS KEY MAP

Major Road
Paved Road
Dirt Road
(most not shown)
Town/Village
Road dead end
Regional Center
Delaware River
Body of Water

0 1 2 3 4
MILES

N

TRAIL REGIONS

DWG -- Pennsylvania
DWG -- New Jersey
Sunfish Pond
Mohican Outdoor Center
Millbrook
Crater Lake
Walpack
Stokes S.F., Southwest
Stony Lake, Southwest
Stony Lake, Northeast
Steam Mill Camp
High Point Southwest
High Point Monument

uniform. Some exceptions are noted on the appropriate individual map. A general legend for maps and profiles is also shown on page 23.

The New York-New Jersey Trail Conference map set "Kittatinny Trails" is a useful companion to this guide. See the reference section for details.

DEFINITIONS

Descriptions

Due to long human habitation of the entire area, there are literally hundreds of woods roads, road remnants, paths, shortcuts, and abandoned trails in these hills. This guide describes only hiking trails which are routinely maintained by an individual or organization (usually a hiking club). The maintaining group is noted in each trail description. Also, almost all of the trails described are blazed. For the few trails where this is not the case, it is so noted. All trails which are known to be routinely maintained and blazed are included in the guide. All of the described trails are sanctioned by either the National Park Service or New Jersey Forest Service or New Jersey Park System. The detailed trail maps often show as dashed lines major woods roads or paths which are not maintained. Maintained trails are shown as solid lines (some of which may be maintained as fire roads).

Certain words and phrases are used repeatedly in the trail descriptions. Exact definitions of the author's usage may be helpful.

Gentle Slope	less than 2% or 100 feet per mile
Moderate Slope	2% to 7% or 100 to 300 feet per mile
Steep Slope	greater than 7% or 300 feet per mile
Rock Scramble	steep enough so that most people will use all fours
Rock Climbing	none of the trails described involve rock climbing
Open Hardwood Forest	generally mature forest with low levels of underbrush
Overgrown Field	A field abandoned between ten and 80 years ago which is reverting to hardwood/conifer forest, often with almost impenetrable underbrush.

Woods Road	Usually an old unimproved road established originally to facilitate logging and/or field access. Age, recent use, and erosion determine width and surface quality.
Woods Path	A narrow path never intended for vehicular traffic. May be old or new, high quality or barely passable.
Smooth Trail	Less than 20% stone covered and little or no erosion.
Unmarked Trail	No consistent blazing. Some may be spray paint marked by individuals trying not to get lost on unsanctioned trails.
Stony Surface	
completely	90+% stone covered
heavily	50 to 90% stone covered
moderately	20 to 50% stone covered
lightly	less than 20% stone covered

Trail lengths are by GPS and quoted to the nearest 0.05 mile.

Commonly Used Abbreviations and Acronyms

AMC	Appalachian Mountain Club
AT	Appalachian Trail
CO	county
DWG	Delaware Water Gap
DWGNRA	Delaware Water Gap National Recreation Area
FT	feet
HPSP	High Point State Forest
I	interstate
MI	miles
NPS	National Park Service
NJ	New Jersey
NYNJTC	New York-New Jersey Trail Conference

N, S, E, W, NW, NE, SW, SE   points of the compass
PA   Pennsylvania
SSF   Stokes State Forest
WSF   Worthington State Forest
c.   circa, about
BCE   Before the Christian Era (BC)
GPS   Global Positioning System
USGS   United States Geological Survey

Definitions of Column Headings for Trail Choice Table on Page 18

1. **Trail Length:** Total length of trail from end to end   — *in [miles]*

2. **Average Slope:** This is the "total climbing" divided by the "trail length." It is a calculated actual average slope, both up slope and down slope, and a good indicator of hiking speed.   — *in [percent]*

3. **Total Climbing:** This includes all ups and downs. Total elevation change encountered whether positive or negative in traveling the trail end to end in either direction.   *(not shown on table).*

4. **Elevation Change: The difference in elevation** between the two ends of the trail.

5. **Scenery/Interest:** Subjective rating of scenery and points of interest on the trail.   *[O = outstanding] [G = good] [F = fair] [L = little]*

6. **Trail Surface:** Subjective rating of difficulty of trail surface based on rock cover, path width, blazing, erosion, stream crossings, wet spots, rock scrambles.   *[E = easy]   [M = moderate]   [D = difficult]   (S) = difficult stream crossing   (R) = short rock scramble*

CHOOSING A TRAIL

To assist the reader in choosing a trail which most closely fits his/her desires and expectations, a table of trail statistics has been compiled and appears below. The statistics listed are indicators of trail difficulty, hiking speed, and other desirability factors.

"Average slope" and "trail surface" have a strong influence on hiking speed. A typical day hiker can do three miles per hour or more with average slopes below 5% on a smooth woods road. On the other hand, a typical hiker on average slopes greater than 15% on a moderate or heavily stoned foot path can be reduced to below one mile per hour.

Total end-to-end elevation change is a strong indicator of the average aerobic level that will be achieved. A 900 foot net climb will produce a lot more heavy breathing than a 900 foot net descent, but the average hiking speed will not be much affected. Going down a steep slope can be as slowing as climbing a steep slope unless the hiker has kamikaze-like feelings toward his/her ankle bones and knees.

Scenery and trail surface ratings are subjective judgments by the author. Rock cover, erosion, path width, steepest sections and stream crossings are all part of the trail surface rating.

Rock scrambles and difficult stream crossings are most relevant to a hiker's capability limits. If a rock scramble or stream crossing is simply too difficult for a hiker, the trail, of course, should be avoided.

Once a trail has been chosen using the table, reading the trail description and inspecting the trail map and elevation profile will provide more detailed information.

COMBINING TRAILS

Inspection of the trail maps in each section will suggest desirable combinations of trails. Most of these will appear in a single region described in this guide, since going from region to region is often a long distance, and mostly the regions are connected only via the AT. Several favorite combination trails are listed on page 22. Many others are possible.

TRAIL CHOOSING GUIDE

Book / Chapter	Trail Name	Length (mi.)	Average Slope (%)	Change in Elev.(ft.)	Trail Surface Rating**	Scenery Rating*	Remarks	Page
	AT-Mt. Minsi	2.1	10.4	950	M(R)	O	Popular trail, great views.	27
DWG-PA (1)	Arrow Is.	0.9	5.9	250	E	G	Winter views, pleasant woods	30
	Slateford	0.9	1.9	80	E	G	Farmland views	32
	Red Dot	1.25	17.9	1180	D(R)	O	Mt. Tammany, great views of gap.	37
	Blue Dot	1.4	13.5	950	M-D	G-O	Mt. Tammany, great views	40
DWG-NJ (2)	Beulaland	1.25	8.3	500	E	F-G	Nice alternate to AT	42
	Holly Sp.	0.4	8.3	150	E	F	Short connector	43
	Karamac	1.1	2.6	100	E	G	Along Delaware Rive above gap	44
	Dunnfield	3.4	5.8	800	M	F-G	Follows Dunnfield Creek	49
	AT/DWG/Sunf.	4.3	5.7	1070	E	G	Popular trail to Sunfish Pond	51
Sunfish Pond (3)	Douglas	1.6	11.8	1000	M	F-G	Short steep way to Sunfish Pond	53
	Garvey Sp.	1.1	18.4	1070	M	F-G	Short steep way to Sunfish Pond	55
	Rock Cores	2.8	7.1	70	E	G	Park brochure & numbered sites	56
	Turquoise	1.1	9.5	130	M-E	F	Partially a fire road, remote.	58

** Subjective Trail Surface Rating: E=Easy M=Moderate D=Difficult (S)=Difficult stream crossing (R)=Short rock scramble

* Subjective Scenery Rating: O=Outstanding G=Good F=Fair L=Little

Book Chapter	Trail Name	Length (mi.)	Average Slope (%)	Change in Elev. (ft.)	Trail Surface Rating**	Scenery Rating*	Remarks	Page
Mohican Center (4)	AT/Sunfi/Camp	4.3	4	280	M	0	Remote, outstanding views	62
	Kaiser Rd.	2	9.6	1020	M	F-G	Climbs Kittatinny Ridge to AT	65
	Coppermines	2	8.5	800	M-E	G	Historic mines, pretty ravine	67
	Rattlesnake	2.2	2.3	260	M-E	F-G	Skirts swamp, parallels AT	69
	AT/Camp/602	3.1	6	150	M-D	0	Spectacular continuous views	71
Millbrook (5)	VanCampers	1.65	3.9	210	M-E(R)	0	Beautiful cascades in ravine	76
	Orchard	0.65	5	200	E	F	Short and pleasant near village	77
	Hamilton Rdge.	2.7	3.8	530	E	F	Old municipal road, part paved	80
	Pioneer	2.2	4	390	E	G	Partly along Delaware River	82
Crater Lake (6)	AT/602/BMLR	3.85	3.3	90	M-E	0	Lots of Valley Views	86
	Crater Lake	1.65	7.8	240	M-E	G-0	Beautiful Glacial Lakes	89
	AT/BMLR/Brnk	7	1.7	90	M	G-0	Ridge top, some good views	92
	Buttermilk Falls	1.6	15	1160	M	0	NJ's highest waterfall	95
Walpack (7)	Walpack Ridge	2.55	3.8	160	E	G	Trail to Thunder Mt. Craft Cntr.	100
	Military Rd.	1.15	7.4	100	E	F-G	Walpack to VanCampen Inn	102
	Tillmans Ravine	0.95	8.7	330	M	G-0	Small cascading brook in ravine	105

Book Chapter	Trail Name	Length (mi.)	Average Slope (%)	Change in Elev. (ft.)	Trail Surface Rating**	Scenery Rating*	Remarks	Page
Stokes SF (8)	Stoll	0.6	2.8	80	E	F-G	Pleasant woods and stream	111
	Shay	1.4	4.7	280	M	F	Mostly a dirt, eroded 4WD road	112
	Steffen	1.75	5.6	280	E	F-G	Easy trail in pleasant wood	113
Southwest	Ladder	0.45	9.1	200	M(S)	G	Steffen tr. to AT, short and steep	115
	AT/Bmk/Culvr	5.5	4.9	360	M	0	Many spectacular views	117
	Acropolis	0.55	12.4	360	E	G	Short, steep wide woods road	120
	Station	0.45	2.1	LOOP	E	F-G	Connects Parking lot to 4 trails	124
Stony Lake	Coursen	1.2	2.9	10	M-E	F-G	Forest trail, Station to Sunrise Rd.	125
	Tower	1.45	2.9	580	M-D(R)(S)	0	Station tr. to Culver Tower on AT	127
Southwest (9)	Stony Brook	1.45	6.8	400	M-D(S)	G	Follows Stony Brook to AT	129
	Lackner	2.2	4.1	60	E	F-G	Easy trail Stony Lake to Park HQ	132
	Lead Mine	0.6	5.4	170	E	F-G	Spur off the Lackner to Crsen. Rd.	133
	Tibbs	0.5	5.8	120	E-M(S)	F	Coursen Rd. to Shotwell Camp.	134
	Swenson	3.95	3.4	200	M	F-G	Long and varied but easy overall	138
Stony Lake	Silver Mine	2.1	3.7	20	E/D	G	First easy woods path, later hard	140
	Blue Mt.	1.4	2.3	50	E	F-G	Easy path in pleasant woods	143
Northeast	Tinsley	1.95	6.9	650	E	G	Skellinger Rd. to AT nr Sunrise Mt.	145
(10)	Spring Cabin	0.3	1.3	0	E	F	Gravel road Tinsley to Swenson	147
	Cartwright	1.25	8.6	550	D(S)(R)	F-G	A very difficult trail overall	148
	AT/Culvr/Deckr	7	5.8	180	M	0	Super ridgetop views, some climbs	151

Book Chapter	Trail Name	Length (mi.)	Average Slope (%)	Change in Elev.(ft.)	Trail Surface Rating**	Scenery Rating*	Remarks	Page
	Steam Mill	0.8	2.4	30	M	F	Along Big Flat Brk. and old fields	157
	Howell	2.7	4.6	230	E-M	F-G	All woods roads, many bridges	158
Steam	Criss	2.25	4.8	130	M	F-G	Gentle slopes in mature hardwood	160
Mill	Deep Root	1.25	6.2	390	E-D	F-G	Easy woods rd. to steep stony path	162
Camp	Rock Oak	1.5	4.4	10	E	F-G	Easy trail in old logged hardwoods	165
(11)	Parker	3.7	2.7	300	E-M(S)	F-G	Woods road, gradual slopes	167
	Iris Trail	4.3	4	160	E	G	Long easy trail parallels AT	173
High	AT/Deckr/NJ23	4.6	5.9	190	M	G-O	Up and down several small ridges	175
Point	Mashipacong	2.6	4.4	300	F-G-E	G	Varied with five distinct pieces	178
Southwest	Blue Dot	0.4	16.2	340	D(R)	G	Steep climb - Sawmill Pd. to AT	181
(12)	Ayers	1	2.7	120	E	F-G	A pleasant walk in the woods	182
	Fuller	0.85	4	20	E	F-G	A short woods walk	183
	Life	0.75	3.8	30	E	F-G	A short pleasant woods path	184
	AT/NJ23/Monu	1.1	3.4	120	M	O	Outstanding view from platform	188
High Point	Monument	3.55	6.6	LOOP	M-E	O	Popular trail with great views	190
Monument	Steeny Kill	0.7	3.6	120	M-E	G	Steeny Kill dam to Monument trail	193
(13)	Old Trail	0.5	5.6	150	E	F-G	Short trail in pleasant mature wood	194
	Kuser Trail	1.9	0.8	60	E	O	Smooth, flat in cedar swamp	195

Commonly Combined Trails

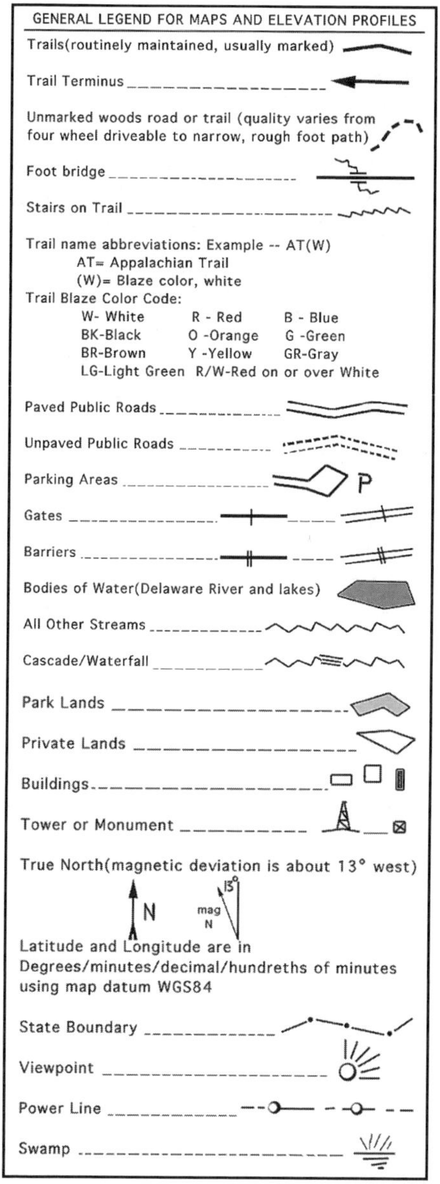

GENERAL LEGEND FOR MAPS AND ELEVATION PROFILES

Trails(routinely maintained, usually marked) ____

Trail Terminus _____

Unmarked woods road or trail (quality varies from
four wheel driveable to narrow, rough foot path)

Foot bridge _____

Stairs on Trail _____

Trail name abbreviations: Example -- AT(W)
    AT= Appalachian Trail
    (W)= Blaze color, white
Trail Blaze Color Code:
      W- White   R - Red   B - Blue
      BK-Black   O -Orange   G -Green
      BR-Brown   Y -Yellow   GR-Gray
      LG-Light Green R/W-Red on or over White

Paved Public Roads _____

Unpaved Public Roads _____

Parking Areas _____ P

Gates _____

Barriers _____

Bodies of Water(Delaware River and lakes)

All Other Streams _____

Cascade/Waterfall _____

Park Lands _____

Private Lands _____

Buildings._____

Tower or Monument _____

True North(magnetic deviation is about 13° west)

N   mag
       N

Latitude and Longitude are in
Degrees/minutes/decimal/hundreths of minutes
using map datum WGS84

State Boundary _____

Viewpoint _____

Power Line _____

Swamp _____

Arrow Island Trail in winter

CHAPTER 1

DELAWARE WATER GAP
TRAILS - PENNSYLVANIA

Delaware Water Gap Trails, Pennsylvania
(DWGNRA)

• Mount Minsi Portion of AT / *2.1 miles*
• Arrow Island Trail / *0.9 mile*
• Slateford Trails / *2.65 miles*

This small part of the Delaware Water Gap National Recreation Area (DWGNRA) on the Pennsylvania side of the Gap is included here because through its geological continuity and its connection with the Appalachian Trail (AT) it forms an integral unit with the New Jersey side of the river. All other trails in this guide are in New Jersey.

Three trails are described here: the Mount Minsi Trail section of the AT which climbs the southwest side of the Water Gap, the Arrow Island Trail which traverses the lower slopes of Mount Minsi, and the Slateford Trail which includes the Slateford Farm and historic site preserved by the National Recreation Area.

Other Pennsylvania trails of the DWGNRA are relatively isolated from the Delaware Water Gap and the Kittatinny range by the Delaware River. The nearest other Pennsylvania DWGNRA trail is about 15 miles north of the Water Gap.

This trail section can be reached on PA State Route 611 from either the north or south. Interstate 80 has an exit onto PA State Route 611 immediately after crossing the bridge into Pennsylvania.

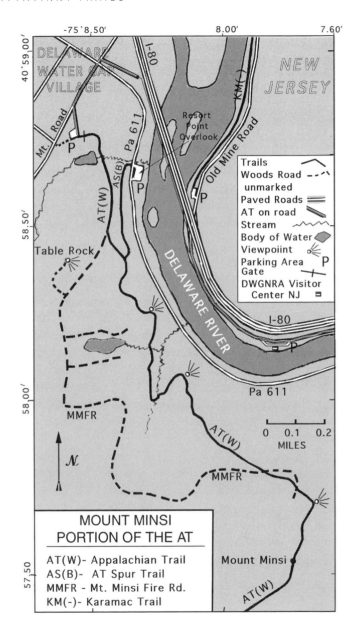

Mount Minsi Portion of the AT   *2.1 miles, white blazed*

General Description

Standing on the uppermost viewpoint on the Mount Minsi trail is a very uplifting experience. Before you stretches the Great Valley of the Appalachians, interspersed with small hills of solid slate and ending ten miles to the southeast in a 500 foot wall of limestone which marks the beginning of the Appalachian Highlands.

The AT at this point folds back upon itself, crossing the Delaware River on the I-80 bridge and following Old Mine Road for a short stretch past the DWGNRA Visitor Center before re-entering the forest at Dunnfield Creek. You can see it below you along the river a quarter mile in the distance as the crow flies, assuming the crow flies horizontally.

Magnificent in any season is not an exaggeration for this portion of the AT.

The actual Mount Minsi summit is 0.2 mile beyond the uppermost viewpoint. In the downhill direction the trail generally parallels the Delaware River. There are several good viewpoints as the trail descends the north face of the mountain down to the outskirts of the village of Delaware Water Gap.

Access

There is ample parking for access to this portion of the AT at an area just off Mountain Road at the edge of Delaware Water Gap village. From PA State

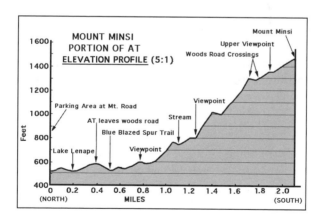

Mount Minsi from Arrow Island Overlook

Route 611 north take the first left after the Resort Point Overlook onto Mountain Road. In one block turn left again. The parking area is on the right. The AT south (toward Mount Minsi) is directly ahead, contiguous with the Mount Minsi Fire Road at this point. You shortly cross the dam of little Lake Lenape.

After 0.4 mile the AT veers left off the fire road into the woods. Another 0.1 mile beyond is an intersection with the blue blazed spur trail to the left. This trail leads in 0.4 mile to the Resort Point Overlook off PA State Route 611, an alternative access point with ample parking. Starting at Resort Point increases the climb to the top by about 100 feet.

Trail Surface

For the first 0.4 mile, the trail is contiguous with the broad, smooth Mount Minsi Fire Road. Beyond, the trail becomes a typical narrow footpath, easy to negotiate for most of its length, but with a few rocky and steep portions almost requiring short scrambles. The trail crosses the fire road twice more near the top, just before the upper viewpoint. The fire road can be used as an alternate trail to the summit. It is unmarked, but easy to follow. The AT and fire road combined make a nice loop hike.

Scenery/Points of Interest

The outstanding viewpoints are the chief attraction of this popular trail segment.

The Table Rock viewpoint can be accessed via the Mount Minsi Fire Road.

Instead of following the AT as it veers left into the woods at 0.4 mile, continue straight on the fire road to a side trail at 0.55 mile from the Mountain Road parking area. Table Rock is 0.15 mile beyond.

Resort Point Overlook is at the site of an old resort hotel, of which some remnants remain.

If you follow the AT's white blazes beyond the Mountain Road parking area (north) you will first traverse a couple of village streets and then cross the Delaware River on a well protected walkway alongside Interstate 80. The fast flowing river below, the surrounding peaks 1200 feet above, and the interstate truck traffic whizzing by at 60 mph create a very dramatic effect. Interesting, but definitely not peaceful. The contrast with the Mount Minsi trail is amazing. No vehicle has ever jumped the barrier between the walkway and the bridge to my knowledge.

Climbing

The total climb between the Mountain Road parking area and the summit of Mount Minsi is 920 feet. Mount Minsi peaks at 1460 above sea level, 1200 feet above the Delaware River. There is very little downhill walking from Mountain Road to the top. It is almost continuously up.

Starting at the Resort Point Overlook shortens the trip by 0.1 mile and increases the climb by 100 feet.

Table Rock is about 170 feet above the Mountain Road parking area.

Maintained by: Wilmington Trail Club.
Permitted Uses: Hiking (understood to include snowshoeing).

Arrow Island Trail

0.9 mile, white blaze

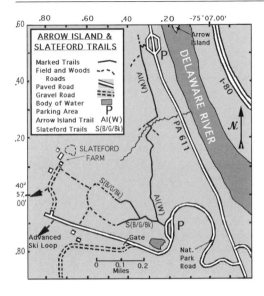

General Description

A short pleasant trail, Arrow Island runs between the Arrow Island Overlook off PA State Route 611 and the parking area on National Park Road prior to reaching Slateford Farm.

For about 400 feet, it is contiguous with the Slateford Trail at the National Park Road end. There are pleasant winter views of Mount Tammany across the river.

The trail was originally blue blazed, but is now white blazed. A few dim blue marks are still evident.

Access

There is ample parking at both ends. The National Park Road parking area is 0.65 mile from the intersection with PA State Route 611 and 0.2 mile short of the Slateford Farm gate.

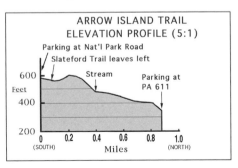

Arrow Island and Slateford Trails intersection

Trail Surface

The trail surface is chiefly on old woods roads of varying quality but generally very easy going. Short steep portions just before a small stream crossing and just before reaching the Arrow Island parking area require some care, but no scrambling.

Scenery

A beautiful open hardwood forest complements good winter views of Mount Tammany in New Jersey across the Delaware River.

Climbing

There is a total drop of 250 feet from the National Park Road end to the Arrow Island Overlook end.

Maintained by: Appalachian Mountain Club.
Permitted Uses: Hiking.

Slateford Trails
2.65 miles, blue, black, red diamond blazed

General Description

The Slateford Trails are designed as cross-country ski trails in three loops. The longest loop is about 2.65 miles. The loops are marked, but difficult to follow in some places. Several pieces of the trail, especially the longest loop, are at the edges of working fields.

The accompanying map (page 30) and elevation profile highlight a good hiking portion of the ski loops from the National Park Road parking area to the Slateford Farm.

Because they are designed as cross-country ski trails, they are generally flat and broad, either on woods roads, on paved roads, or on field edges.

Slateford Farm

The Slateford Farm can be reached from the National Park Road parking area in 0.9 mile.

The first 400 feet is contiguous with the Arrow Island Trail. The Slateford Trail then veers left on a woods road. At 0.15 mile the trail splits right and left, marked the same in both directions. Take the left fork which soon ends in a working field. Follow the right edge of the field to another woods road. Take this road to the left. At 0.45 mile this road intersects the newly paved approach road to Slateford Farm. Turn right on this road to its end at 0.6 mile and continue on the gravel drive to the farmstead at 0.9 mile.

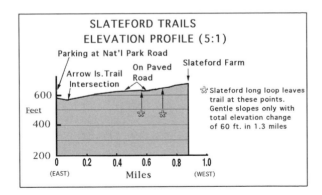

Slateford Farm with Hercules Hound

You can return to the parking area by following the paved drive back to National Park Road and turning left (0.2 mile on National Park Road).

The Slateford Farm is a preserved slate mining operation. The buildings are often closed, but a tour of the exterior and of the slate pit is interesting.

Maintained by: Appalachian Mountain Club.
Permitted Uses: Hiking and cross-country skiing.

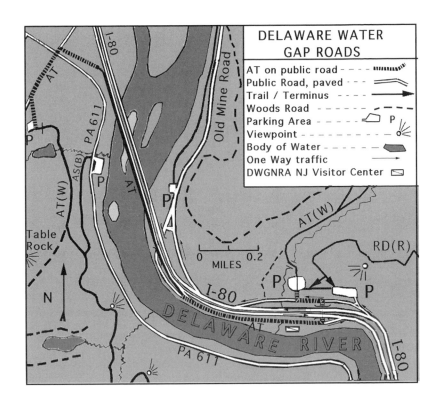

DELAWARE WATER
GAP ROADS

AT on public road - - - - ᴹᴹᴹᴹᴹᴹᴹ
Public Road, paved - - - ⟹
Trail / Terminus   - - - - ➤
Woods Road   - - - - - -
Parking Area - - - - - - ⬭ P
Viewpoint - - - - - - - - - ◌
Body of Water - - - - - ⬛
One Way traffic   ➝
DWGNRA NJ Visitor Center ⬒

CHAPTER 2

DELAWARE WATER GAP
TRAILS- NEW JERSEY

Delaware Water Gap Trails, New Jersey
(WSF)

- Red Dot Trail (Mt. Tammany) / *1.2 miles*
- Blue Dot Trail (Mt. Tammany) / *2.1 miles*
- Beulaland Trail / *1.25 miles*
- Holly Springs / *0.4 mile*
- Karamac Trail / *1.1 miles*

The New Jersey side of the Delaware Water Gap can be reached via Interstate 80. There are two exits going west, the first for the Dunnfield parking areas and a quarter-mile beyond for Old Mine Road just before the bridge over the river to Pennsylvania. Going east, there is an exit onto Old Mine Road immediately after the bridge over the Delaware. The Dunnfield parking areas can also be reached by taking the Old Mine Road south to its end and crossing under I-80.

The DWGNRA New Jersey Visitor Center just off Old Mine Road at the Gap is worth a visit. A detailed map of Delaware Water Gap roads is shown opposite. The Red Dot Trail, the Blue Dot Trail and the AT to Sunfish Pond all start at the Dunnfield parking areas. The AT and Dunnfield Creek trails are described in the following section under "Sunfish Pond Trails".

Parking areas for the Karamac and Beulaland trails are on Old Mine Road about one mile from I-80. All of these trails are chiefly within New Jersey's Worthington State Forest. They are among the most popular trails in the entire Kittatinny range.

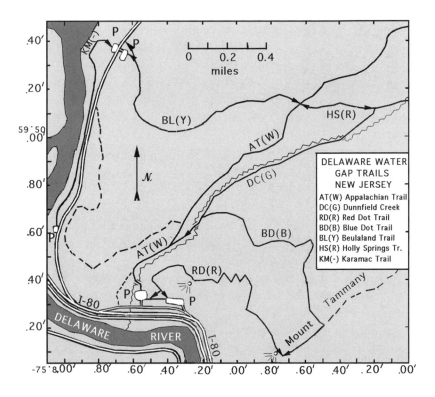

The AT crossing the Delaware

Red Dot Trail
1.2 miles, red dot on white square blazed

General Description

The Red Dot Trail is one of two trails which climb to the top of Mount Tammany from the Dunnfield parking areas. The Dunnfield parking areas are in the heart of the Delaware Water Gap just off Interstate 80 westbound and just prior to the I-80 toll bridge which crosses into Pennsylvania. Mount Tammany is the high point on the New Jersey side of the Water Gap. It's New Jersey's equivalent to Mount Minsi which is described in the previous section. The other Mount Tammany trail is the Blue Dot Trail, described on pages 40-41.

The Red Dot Trail is relatively difficult. It climbs from the Gap almost directly up the north face of Mount Tammany. The north face is the most gradual route but still quite steep, rising about 1100 feet in about 1.2 miles. Excellent Water Gap viewpoints exist about 1/3 of the way to the top and at the top.

Access

At the Water Gap end, two Red Dot Trail spurs head from the two Dunnfield parking areas. They join each other in less than a tenth of a mile. A connector

Mount Minsi and the Great Valley from the Mt. Tammany Upper Viewpoint

trail from the first to the second parking area has also been established.

In addition to the two paved parking areas which are about 0.1 mile apart, there is also an overflow grassy parking area beyond the second lot. The Red Dot Trail does not directly connect to this parking area. The Dunnfield parking areas are very popular at times because they are a scenic rest stop for I-80 travelers and because the major trails accessing Mount Tammany and Sunfish Pond, including the AT, start here.

Near the top of Mount Tammany, the Red Dot Trail connects directly to the Blue Dot Trail (see pages 40-41). Most people climb up one and down the other. The Blue Dot Trail is a bit longer and a bit more gradual.

Trail Surface

In places, stairways have been established by the trail maintainers out of wood or stone. In other areas, some rock scrambling is required. The trail improvement work continues. About half the trail is steep enough to require either stairs or scrambles. The other half is stony woods path. There are no significant wet spots or stream crossings.

Scenery/Points of Interest

Spectacular views of the Water Gap exist at two locations on the trail. The scenery at the Dunnfield parking areas is also remarkable. In addition to the viewpoints shown on the map, lesser, more restricted views are available from about 1/3 of the trail.

For those not interested in climbing all the way to the top, the lower viewpoint, about 500 feet above the Delaware River, is worth a journey.

Climbing

The trail is steep, rising about 1150 feet in little more than 1.2 miles. That is an average slope of 18%. In several places, there are short slopes in excess of 50% (0.5 feet per foot). No rock climbing is required, however.

Maintained by: New York-New Jersey Trail Conference.
Permitted Uses: Hiking only.

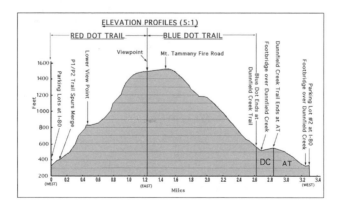

Blue Dot Trail
1.4 miles, blue dot on white square blazed

General Description (map on p. 36)

The Blue Dot Trail climbs the same mountain, Mount Tammany, as the Red Dot Trail, but does it in 1.4 miles, rather than 1.2 miles. So it is a bit more gradual. The trail is mostly east of the Red Dot Trail and therefore a bit removed from the Water Gap. There are no Water Gap views except from the top.

Starting at the end of the Red Dot Trail, the trail traverses 0.3 mile of the Mount Tammany ridge line before turning left down the north face of Mount Tammany. At 1.4 miles the trail merges with the Dunnfield Creek Trail. The Dunnfield Creek Trail and the AT can be used to return to the Dunnfield parking areas in 0.7 mile when doing a Red Dot/Blue Dot loop hike. Total distance is 3.3 mi. See the elevation profiles.

The trail is in hardwood forest most of its length. At the top of Mount Tammany the trees are stunted, almost scrub-like. At the Dunnfield Creek end, hemlocks become more frequent.

Mount Tammany from Arrow Island Overlook

Access

The Red Dot Trail directly connects to the Blue Dot Trail at the high Water Gap viewpoint near the summit of Mount Tammany.

The Blue Dot Trail merges with the Dunnfield Creek Trail about 1/4-mile from where the two trails start at the AT. The AT south, in turn, runs to the second Dunnfield Creek parking area off I-80.

If either the Dunnfield Creek Trail or the AT is taken to the right when descending from Mount Tammany (instead of to the left), Sunfish Pond will be reached in about three miles.

Trail Surface

For most of its length, the Blue Dot Trail is a stony woods path with little or no rock scrambling required. At the top of the Mount Tammany ridge line, the trail is broader and less stony for 0.35 mile.

Scenery/Points of Interest

There are spectacular views of the Water Gap where the trail joins the Red Dot Trail and also of the Great Valley of the Appalachians in New Jersey all along the Mount Tammany ridge line.

Climbing

From the Dunnfield Creek Trail to the top of the Mount Tammany ridge line is about a 1000 foot climb. A gradual downward slope follows to the junction with the Red Dot Trail. The AT portion from the Dunnfield parking areas to the Dunnfield Creek Trail climbs about 200 feet (see elevation profile on p. 39).

Maintained by: New York-New Jersey Trail Conference.
Permitted Uses: Hiking only.

Beulaland Trail (Farview Trail)   *1.25 miles, yellow blazed*

General Description (*map on p. 36*)

An alternate route to Sunfish Pond, the Beulaland Trail begins on Old Mine Road at the Farview parking area just 1.4 miles from I-80. After a relatively gentle climb, it intersects the AT at 1.25 miles. It is also known as the Farview Trail in WSF brochures. DWGNRA publications and all other known publications and maps identify the trail as the Beulaland.

Access

The trail is accessible from Old Mine Road. From I-80, take the last exit in New Jersey just before crossing the toll bridge to Pennsylvania, staying right to enter Old Mine Road. The first half-mile is a one-lane corniche road along the Delaware River so traffic is limited to one direction at a time by a set of very long traffic lights. At 1.4 miles from I-80 you will see the Farview parking area on the right and the Karamac parking area on the left. The Beulaland Trail terminates at the north end of the Farview lot. A signpost at the trailhead identifies the trail as the Farview.

The other end of the Beulaland is a trail crossroads. The AT goes left or right, and straight ahead is the Holly Springs Trail. Take the AT left to get to Sunfish Pond (2.2 miles) or right to get to the Dunnfield parking areas at I-80 (1.5 miles). The Holly Springs Trail intersects the Dunnfield Creek Trail about 0.4 mile beyond the trail crossroads.

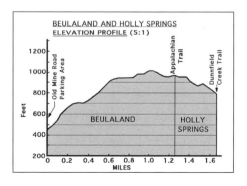

Trail Surface
The Beulaland Trail is a gentle old woods road for most of its length.

Scenery/Points of Interest
An alternate route to Sunfish Pond.

Climbing
There is a 550 foot elevation gain from Old Mine Road to the top of the ridge. The AT is encountered about 50 feet below the ridge top.

Maintained by: New York-New Jersey Trail Conference.
Permitted Uses: Hiking only.

Holly Springs Trail   *0.4 mile, red blazed*

General Description (map on p. 36)
This short trail connects the AT with the Dunnfield Creek Trail. The AT, Holly Springs and Dunnfield Creek trails form a popular three mile loop out of the Dunnfield parking areas of I-80 at the Delaware Water Gap.

Access
The trail runs from the AT, where it is essentially a continuation of the Beulaland Trail, to the Dunnfield Creek Trail.

Trail Surface
Grassy woods road.

Scenery/Points of Interest
The Holly Spring is about midway on the trail.

Climbing
There is a drop of a little less than 200 feet from the AT to the Dunnfield Creek Trail.

43

Maintained by: New York-New Jersey Trail Conference.
Permitted Uses: Hiking only.

Karamac Trail

1.1 miles, unblazed

General Description *(map on p. 36)*

The Karamac Trail snakes along the New Jersey side of the Delaware River on the north side of the Water Gap. It lies between a corniche road portion of Old Mine Road and the river for most of its length, following an old railroad bed. Where the old railroad bed started to cross the river (0.9 mile from the south end), the trail veers right and climbs through the hardwood forest up to the Karamac parking area off Old Mine Road.

Access

There is parking for two or three cars at the south end off Old Mine Road in the shadow of the I-80 bridge over the Delaware. There is ample parking at the Karamac parking area 1.2 miles beyond and opposite the Farview parking area where the Beulaland Trail begins.

Trail Surface

For most of its length an old railroad bed is followed. The northern 0.2 mile is a narrow but smooth footpath. The unmarked trail is a bit difficult to follow at the northern end since several spur trails have been established leading nowhere.

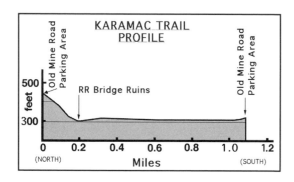

44

Old Mine Road above the Karamac Trail in Winter

Scenery

The trail is mostly on a bluff above the Delaware River with views across the river to Pennsylvania.

Climbing

A climb of 150 feet from the railroad bridge abutment to the Karamac parking area is required.

Maintained by: Appalachian Mountain Club.
Permitted Uses: Hiking.

Junco

CHAPTER 3

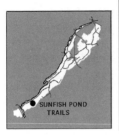

Sunfish Pond Trails (DWGNRA/WSF)

- Dunnfield Creek Trail / *3.4 miles*
- AT Water Gap to Sunfish Pond / *4.3 miles*
- Douglas Trail / *1.65 miles*
- Garvey Springs Trail / *1.15 miles*
- Rock Cores Trail / *2.85 miles*
- Turquoise Trail / *1.1 miles*

Sunfish Pond, a glacial lake 1,000 feet above the surrounding valleys, is one of the more popular destinations of day hikers on the Kittatinny Ridge. There are six ways to get there.

The Dunnfield Creek Trail and the AT are accessible from the Dunnfield parking areas at the Water Gap. The Douglas Trail and Garvey Springs Trail trailheads are close together across Old Mine Road from a large parking area. The Turquoise Trail connects the Sunfish Pond Fire Road with the AT to complete a circumnavigation of Sunfish Pond, and a spur leads from the Sunfish Pond Fire Road to the Mount Tammany Fire Road. Neither fire road is routinely maintained as a trail, nor are they blazed. One can also reach Sunfish Pond by going south on the AT starting at Camp Road (see Chapter 4 p. 62).

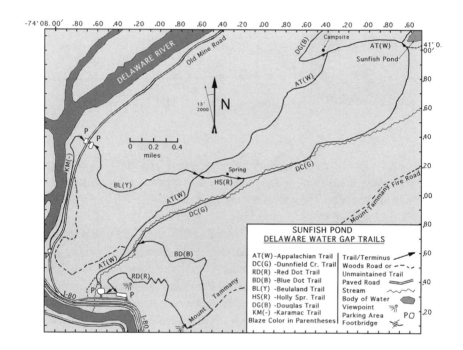

-74°08.00′ .80 .60 .40 .20 .00 .80 .60 .40 .20 .00 .80 .60 .40 .20 .00 .80 .60

DELAWARE RIVER

Old Mine Road

DG(B)   Campsite   AT(W)
Sunfish Pond

AT(W)

13′
2000
N

P
P

0   0.2   0.4
miles

KM(-)

Spring

BL(Y)   HS(R)   DC(G)

AT(W)   DC(G)

Mount Tammany Fire Road

BD(B)

AT(W)

RD(R)

P
P

I-80

I-80

Mount Tammany

SUNFISH POND
DELAWARE WATER GAP TRAILS

AT(W) -Appalachian Trail	Trail/Terminus
DC(G) -Dunnfield Cr. Trail	Woods Road or - - -
RD(R) -Red Dot Trail	Unmaintained Trail
BD(B) -Blue Dot Trail	Paved Road
BL(Y) -Beulaland Trail	Stream
HS(R) -Holly Spr. Trail	Body of Water
DG(B) -Douglas Trail	Viewpoint
KM(-) -Karamac Trail	Parking Area P
Blaze Color in Parentheses	Footbridge

41° 0.
00′
.80
.60
.40
.20
.00
.80
.60
.40
.20

48

Dunnfield Creek Trail   *3.4 miles, green blazed*

General Description

One of two trails from the Water Gap to Sunfish Pond, the Dunnfield Creek Trail branches right off of the AT at 0.4 mile from the Dunnfield parking areas at I-80. It follows Dunnfield Creek, crossing it at several points, for most of its length (about 2.8 miles) and then veers left away from the stream climbing 350 feet to a ridge line a little above Sunfish Pond. At 3.4 miles, the trail terminates at the AT again, only a few hundred feet from Sunfish Pond.

Access

The AT, starting at the second Dunnfield parking area, follows Dunnfield Creek on a broad, well traveled woods road. At 0.4 mile from the parking area, the AT climbs away from the creek to the left. At this point the Dunnfield Creek Trail veers to the right to stay with the stream. It crosses the stream about six times, the first three on foot bridges. The other crossings are far enough upstream so that stepping-stone crossings are usually not a problem.

At 1.3 miles from the southwest end of the Dunnfield Creek Trail the Holly Springs Trail intersects from the left. This short trail (0.4 mile) takes you back to the AT. A left hand turn at the AT will bring you back to the Dunnfield parking area for a total 2.5 miles loop hike.

Continuing beyond the Holly Springs Trail, there are no other trail intersections until just before you reach Sunfish Pond and the northeast terminus of the trail. The Sunfish Pond Fire Road, unmarked, leaves to the right just

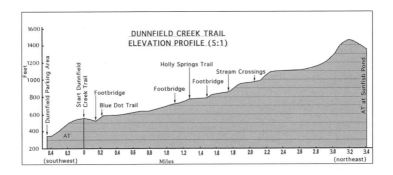

49

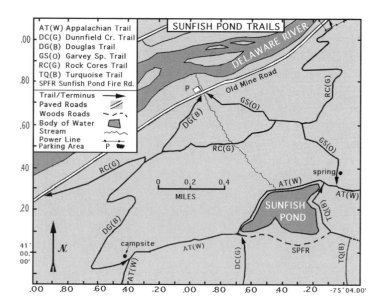

SUNFISH POND TRAILS

AT(W) Appalachian Trail
DC(G) Dunnfield Cr. Trail
DG(B) Douglas Trail
GS(O) Garvey Sp. Trail
RC(G) Rock Cores Trail
TQ(B) Turquoise Trail
SPFR Sunfish Pond Fire Rd.

Trail/Terminus
Paved Roads
Woods Roads
Body of Water
Stream
Power Line
Parking Area   P

prior to the trail terminus at the AT. A right turn at either the fire road or the AT will lead around Sunfish Pond, the fire road on the southeast shore and the AT on the northwest shore. A return to the Dunnfield parking area from the trail terminus yields a total round trip of 7.5 miles.

Trail Surface

The southwest end of the trail is on a broad, fairly smooth woods road. Beyond the Holly Springs intersection, it becomes more and more narrow and more and more stony. During times of high water there are several wet spots. Eventually the trail becomes somewhat indistinct requiring some attention to follow it. The final piece which climbs the ridge to the left of the creek (looking upstream) is more distinct and smoother again.

Scenery/Points of Interest

For most of the trail length you will be in mixed hardwood and hemlock forest. Somewhat stunted hardwood forest as well as some forest fire damage prevails on the rise at the northeast end of the trail.

Sunfish Pond is a well known attraction. It remains quite isolated and pristine since it is accessible only on foot, and only by climbing about 1000 feet.

Climbing

The total climb from the Dunnfield parking area to Sunfish Pond is a little over 1000 feet. It is in three parts: (1)The AT from I-80 to the Dunnfield Creek Trail trailhead, 200 feet; (2) The Dunnfield Creek Trail, following the creek, climbs 550 feet before turning left to climb the final ridge; (3) The final ridge, the steepest climb on the trail, is about 350 feet followed by a drop of 100 feet down to Sunfish Pond.

Maintained by: New York-New Jersey Trail Conference.
Permitted Uses: Hiking only.

AT: Water Gap to Sunfish Pond   *4.3 miles, white blazed*

General Description *(map on p. 48)*

After crossing the Delaware River from Pennsylvania on the I-80 bridge (see Mount Minsi Trail), the AT follows Old Mine Road to its end at the Dunnfield parking areas. The Old Mine Road crosses under I-80 from north to south and ends at a one way short service road which accesses the Dunnfield parking areas.

The AT re-enters the forest on the north side of the second Dunnfield parking lot. It quickly crosses Dunnfield Creek on a footbridge and follows

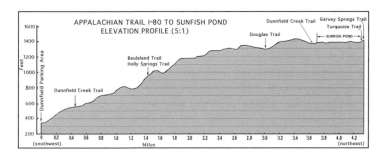

the creek for about a half mile, climbing moderately on a broad woods road. This is perhaps the most popular trail in the Kittatinnies and it shows in the width of the trail and in moderate erosion for most of its length.

After leaving Dunnfield Creek, the trail continues to climb moderately for another half mile and then levels off for

Sunfish Pond

a short stretch before climbing quite steeply just prior to the crossing of the Beulaland/Holly Springs trails at about 1.5 miles from the parking area. Gradual and steep climbs continue to alternate until about 1.9 miles; then the trail becomes more gradual.

The Douglas Trail and the backpacker campground are reached at 3.1 miles from the Dunnfield parking area. On the AT between the Douglas Trail and the Dunnfield Creek Trail just prior to Sunfish Pond at 3.7 miles, a few distant glimpses of the Water Gap are possible in winter months. After passing the Dunnfield Creek Trail, the AT closely follows the northwest shore of Sunfish Pond on a stony woods path. The Garvey Springs Trail enters at 4.3 miles, ending this section of the AT. See Chapter 4 for a description of the Camp Road to Sunfish Pond section.

Access
The following AT access points are described elsewhere:
> Dunnfield Parking Area from the southwest
> Camp Road crossing via AT from the northeast
> Dunnfield Creek Trail (two intersections)
> Beulaland Trail
> Holly Springs Trail
> Douglas Trail

Trail Surface

The AT in this section is a broad woods road with some erosion. There are a few steep sections from Delaware Water Gap to Sunfish Pond. It becomes a narrow, stony woods path along the northwest shore of Sunfish Pond.

Scenery/Points of Interest

Sunfish Pond
Backpacker Campsites
Distant winter views of the Delaware Water Gap
Dunnfield Creek Ravine/Cascades

Climbing

A total climb of 1,100 feet between the Delaware Water Gap and a point just above Sunfish Pond at 3.4 miles from the Gap. Essentially flat thereafter.

Maintained by: New York-New Jersey Trail Conference.
Permitted Uses: Hiking only.

Douglas Trail   *1.65 miles, blue blazed*

General Description *(map on p. 50)*

This is a popular route to Sunfish Pond. It begins on Old Mine Road and climbs moderately on a woods road. The Rock Cores Trail (see below) is

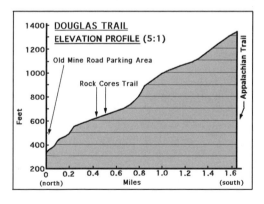

contiguous at 0.45 mile to 0.55 mile from Old Mine Road. After Rock Cores, the trail climbs a bit more steeply with switchbacks on a woods path. At 1.65 miles, the trail terminates at the AT near the backpacker campsite. A left turn onto the AT will bring you to Sunfish Pond in 0.6 mile. A right turn will bring you to the Dunnfield parking areas at the Delaware Water Gap in about 3.0 miles.

Access

The trail starts directly opposite the Douglas parking area across Old Mine Road. The Sunfish Pond runoff stream is to the left. The Rock Cores Trail may be used as a more gradual approach by taking it where it begins on Old Mine Road, just north of the side road to the Worthington State Forest office and campground. The trail may also be accessed from the AT, of course.

A favorite loop hike of 4.3 miles is to take the Douglas Trail up, go left on the AT past Sunfish Pond, and left onto the Garvey Springs Trail.

Trail Surface

A rough old woods road from Old Mine Road to the Rock Cores Trail and a narrower woods path from the Rock Cores Trail to the AT.

Scenery/Points of Interest

Sunfish Pond remains a relatively pristine high glacial lake (elevation, 1100 feet) due to its remote location.

Climbing

An almost continuous climb of 1100 feet from Old Mine Road to the AT.

Maintained by: New York-New Jersey Trail Conference.
Permitted Uses: Hiking only.

Garvey Springs Trail

1.15 miles, orange blazed

General Description *(map on p. 50)*

The Garvey Springs Trail is the shortest route to Sunfish Pond. It climbs steeply from Old Mine Road, rising about 1100 feet in less than 1.2 miles. That's an average grade of 18 percent. The upper end intersects the AT 0.1 mile to the northeast of Sunfish Pond. A right turn onto the AT will bring you to the pond.

The Rock Cores Trail appears on the right about 0.45 mile from Old Mine Road. At 0.6 mile it departs to the left.

Access

There is ample parking at the Douglas Trail lot almost directly across Old Mine Road from the start of the Garvey Springs Trail. The Sunfish Pond runoff stream crosses Old Mine Road at this point. The Garvey Springs Trail begins just to the left (northeast) of the runoff, and the Douglas Trail begins just to the right (southwest).

The Rock Cores Trail is contiguous with the Garvey Springs for about 0.15 mile.

The Garvey Springs Trail terminates at the AT, 0.1 mile north of Sunfish Pond. A popular Sunfish Pond loop is to combine this trail with the Douglas Trail and the AT.

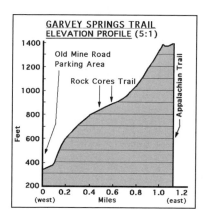

Trail Surface

The trail from Old Mine Road to the Rock Cores Trail is a rough old woods road. Above the Rock Cores Trail it becomes a woods path and is heavily eroded and stony in some sections.

Scenery/Points of Interest

Sunfish Pond is an isolated high glacial lake still in pristine condition due to its remote location and the fact that it can be reached only on foot.

Garvey Spring is just prior to the AT terminus.

Climbing

The trail goes continuously upward, 1100 feet from Old Mine Road to the AT.

Maintained by: New York-New Jersey Trail Conference.
Permitted Uses: Hiking only.

Rock Cores Trail   *2.85 miles, green over white blazed*

General Description *(map on p. 50)*

The Rock Cores Trail is a Worthington State Forest self-guided tour trail which was formerly known as the Northwest Trail. There are 13 numbered sign posts, eight identifying various trees, and the remainder pointing out minor points of interest. A brochure describing the trail and the numbered posts is available from the Worthington State Forest office, which is located in

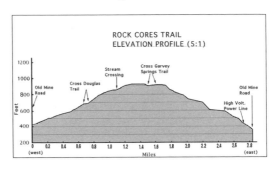

Mt. Tammany from DWGNRA Visitor Center

the main Worthington camp ground about three miles from the Water Gap off Old Mine Road.

The western end of the Rock Cores Trail begins on Old Mine Road less than 0.1 mile beyond the drive to the forest office and main campground. It ascends on a broad but fairly steep woods road to the Douglas Trail, crossing it with a left-right jog (at 0.7 mile). It continues to climb to about 900 feet, then levels out for a short stretch where it crosses the Garvey Springs Trail (at 1.5 miles). It follows the Garvey Springs Trail to the right for about 0.15 mile and then turns left and begins descending. Signpost #11 marks the remains of rock core drilling done to begin the design work on the 160-foot long earthen Tocks Island dam which was, of course, never built. The trail crosses under a power line just before descending steeply back down to Old Mine Road.

Access

No parking is available at the west end of the trail, but it is available at the Worthington State Forest office about 0.6 mile down a paved drive which begins very close to the west end of the trail.

There is parking along Old Mine Road for a few cars about 0.2 mile from the eastern end of the trail.

The trail is also accessible from the Douglas and Garvey Springs trails.

Trail Surface

Broad, moderately stony woods path for most if its length, steep in some places.

Scenery/Points of Interest

Thirteen sign-posted trees and other points of interest including the Tocks Island rock cores. Take care around the rock cores area. Beware of holes in the ground and do not enter.

Climbing

From the western end the trail climbs fairly continuously about 500 feet in 1.2 miles (average slope about 9%). It then levels out for a half mile and descends 500 feet back to Old Mine Road. This descent is more uneven with relatively level and very steep portions alternating.

Maintained by: New Jersey Forest Service.
Permitted Uses: Hiking only.

Turquoise Trail   *1.10 miles, blue blazed*

General Description *(map on p. 50)*

A short section (0.35 mile) of the Turquoise Trail connects the AT to the Sunfish Pond Fire Road to complete the circumferential hike around Sunfish Pond near the east shore. It goes up a bluff overlooking Sunfish Pond, then proceeds across a swampy area, crossing a small inlet stream, then back up a slope to the broad fire road. A short side trail at the bluff leads to a beautiful overview of Sunfish Pond.

The trail then follows the fire road for about 500 feet before turning right toward the Mount Tammany Fire Road. This section descends into the Dunnfield Creek ravine, crossing the brook which is quite small at this point at 0.3 mile from Sunfish Pond Fire Road. It then climbs more gradually back up the Kittatinny Ridge and ends at the Mount Tammany Fire Road at a little over 1.1 miles. The forest is mostly mixed hardwoods, except between the Sunfish Pond Fire Road and Dunnfield Creek where there is new growth in an old forest fire area.

Access

This is one of the more remote trails in Worthington State Forest. It begins at the AT several miles from any road and ends on the unmarked Mount Tammany Fire Road. The fire road can be used to get to Mount Tammany and the Red Dot or Blue Dot trails which are about 2.5 miles to the southwest.

Trail Surface
Moderate to heavily stoned woods path on the northeast side of Sunfish Pond. From Sunfish Pond to Dunnfield Creek the forest service has recently cut a large fire road. Plans are to extend it to the Mount Tammany Fire Road.

Points of Interest
Sunfish Pond

Climbing
There are several climbs (less than 100 feet) on the section following the east shore of Sunfish Pond.

There is a 200 foot descent into the Dunnfield Creek ravine and a 250 foot climb back up to the top of the Kittatinny Ridge and the Mount Tammany Fire Road.

Maintained by: New York-New Jersey Trail Conference.
Permitted Uses: Hiking only.

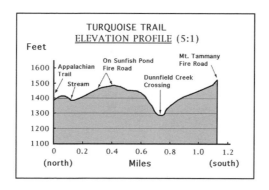

Kittatinny Ridge

CHAPTER 4

MOHICAN OUTDOOR
CENTER TRAILS

Mohican Outdoor Center Trails (DWGNRA)

- AT-Sunfish Pond to Camp Road / *4.3 miles*
- Kaiser Road Trail / *2.0 miles*
- Coppermines Trail / *2.0 miles*
- Rattlesnake Swamp Trail / *2.25 miles*
- AT-Camp Road to NPS 602 / *3.1 miles*

T he Appalachian Mountain Club (AMC) operates the Mohican Outdoor Center within the DWGNRA. There are cabins to rent, a camp store and lodge with a great fireplace, and a beautiful glacial lake, Catfish Pond, only slightly smaller than Sunfish Pond. The AMC also maintains several trails in the DWGNRA in New Jersey and many more in Pennsylvania.

The Mohican Center is accessible by a gravel road, Camp Road. Camp Road begins on Gaisler Road, a paved public road about 1.5 miles from Mohican Center. Gaisler Road, in turn, intersects Warren County RT 602 (becomes NPS 602) about 2.5 miles to the northeast. Overall, it is quite an isolated place.

The AT crosses Camp Road just prior to the camp store and the Coppermines Trail trailhead is less than 100 yards west of Camp Road on the AT. A spur of the Rattlesnake SwampTrail continues from the end of Camp Road about 1/2-mile beyond the camp store. The Kaiser Road Trail trailhead is 1.9 miles southwest of Camp Road on the AT, as well. So the Mohican Outdoor Center is an excellent starting point for hikes in five different directions.

61

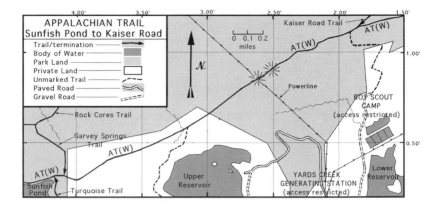

AT-Sunfish Pond to Camp Road

4.3 miles, white blazed

General Description *(see also map on p. 66)*

Sunfish Pond lies on a high, relatively flat plateau-like area. The Kittatinny Ridge at this point does a zig-zag fold upon itself, going northeast, then west, then back to northeast. This fold creates the wide, high, flat spot where Sunfish Pond and the Upper Yards Creek Reservoir lie. To the southwest and northeast the ridge line above 1400 feet is less than 1000 feet wide (0.2 mile), but at the fold it is as wide as 6000 feet (1.15 miles).

The AT traverses the western edge of the fold, first following the north shore of Sunfish Pond, then mounting a low rise toward a stream crossing at 0.85 mile, and finally returning to the narrow southwest to northeast running ridge line, cresting at a high point known as Mount Mohican near the Worthington State Park/Delaware Water Gap National Recreation Area boundary.

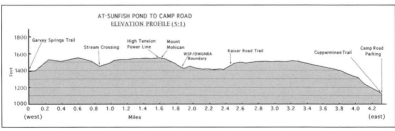

Catfish Pond

Views of the Great Valley open up as the trail crests the Kittatinny Ridge at Mount Mohican and beyond. The trail stays atop the ridge until it drops down to almost 1,100 feet elevation at Camp Road.

Access

Except near the Camp Road end the AT is quite isolated in this segment. Between the Kaiser Road and Garvey Springs trails, the AT is accessible only by climbing 1,000 feet and several miles from the nearest parking area. A good place to go if you want to get away from it all.

There is parking for several cars at the point where it crosses Camp Road.

The Coppermines Trail terminates at the AT just 200 to 300 feet from Camp Road. The only other intersecting trail is the Kaiser Road Trail, 1.9 miles south from Camp Road. Walking south, just after the Kaiser Road Trail, a blue blazed spur trail leads downward to a Boy Scout Camp at the base of the ridge. The scout camp is operating; however, access to and from this camp is strictly controlled at the moment, so it is really not a viable access point.

Trail Surface

A forest foot path for most of its length with a few spots on old woods roads. Heading south, after the Kaiser Road Trail enters from the right, be careful not to stay on the woods road as it veers left off the ridge line. The AT bears right on a stony foot path.

Scenery/Points of Interest

There are excellent, almost continuous views of the Great Valley of the Appalachians to the southeast from the point where the ridge top is achieved about one mile from Camp Road all the way to Mount Mohican (1,480 feet), a distance of about 1-3/4 miles. There are also views of Pennsylvania to the northwest in the area of Mount Mohican.

Yards Creek pumping station and the reservoir lie just to the southeast of the trail. This is a major generating station which stores energy by pumping water up to the upper reservoir in times of low demand, and using that water to run turbines in times of high demand.

Climbing

Heading south from Camp Road the trail climbs 400 feet in one mile to the top of the Kittatinny Ridge. A further 150 foot climb brings you to the top of Mount Mohican at 1480 feet at about 2.5 miles from Camp Road. There are a couple of 100 foot ups and downs before the trail finally descends 200 feet to Sunfish Pond.

Maintained by: New York-New Jersey Trail Conference.
Permitted Uses: Hiking only.

Kaiser Road Trail

2.0 miles, blue blazed

General Description

Named for the Kayser family, local landowners prior to the establishment of the Delaware Water Gap National Recreation Area, the Kaiser Road Trail runs from Old Mine Road to the AT, climbing 1000 feet in two miles with an average slope of 9.6%. There are two connector trails to the Coppermines Trail which very generally parallels the Kaiser Road Trail.

The steepest portion of the trail is at the Old Mine Road end (western) where there is a 15% grade for the first 0.4 mile. It then rises more gradually for the 1.5 miles to the AT.

Blazing is almost non-existent, especially toward the western end of the trail, but because it is an old woods road the entire way, it is relatively easy to follow. The only confusing parts are at a couple of locations where short side roads create a fork, forcing you to make a choice. If you make the wrong choice it soon becomes evident.

The lower connector trail to the Coppermines Trail is also poorly marked.

Access

There is a large parking area on Old Mine Road just to the northeast of the trail head. The AT end is currently quite remote, most easily reachable from Camp Road, which is 1.9 miles north east on the AT.

A connecting trail veers south from the AT about 400 feet to the southwest

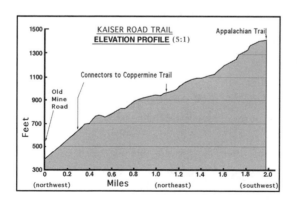

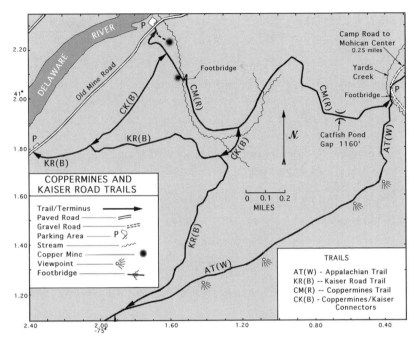

of where the Kaiser Road Trail intersects the AT. It leads to an operating Boy Scout Camp in about 0.7 mile. Access to the camp is restricted by the Yards Creek Generating Station. There is discussion about establishing access to the camp via Gaisler Road (a public road) but this is not yet happening.

The two connectors to the Coppermines Trail can also be used to access the Kaiser Road Trail. The lower connector is about 0.6 mile long and the upper is about 0.2 mile.

Trail Surface
The entire length is an old woods road. There is a fair amount of erosion creating a stony surface, especially in the steeper sections.

Scenery/Points of Interest
There are excellent views of the Great Valley in New Jersey from the AT immediately to the southwest of the intersection with the Kaiser Road Trail.

66

Climbing

From Old Mine Road to the AT is an almost constant climb of close to 1100 feet. The slope is steepest, at close to 15%, in the first 0.4 mile and the last 0.3 mile. Overall average slope is about 10%.

Maintained by: Appalachian Mountain Club.
Permitted Uses: Hiking, cross-country skiing.

Coppermines Trail   *2.0 miles, red blazed*

General Description

This trail runs between Old Mine Road and Camp Road, climbing about 800 feet in less than two miles. Enter the trail across Old Mine Road from the Coppermines parking lot. A short spur trail leads immediately to the left to an old copper mine (about 0.15 mile). Returning to the main trail we climb steeply past some old building foundations and emerge in a short time into a steep sided ravine in hemlock forest. A blue blazed connector trail to the right leads to the Kaiser Road Trail at about 0.25 mile. At 0.4 mile, the trail crosses the stream. There are several interesting cascades. Another old copper mine entrance is to the right of the trail just before crossing the foot bridge. A second blue blazed connector to the Kaiser Road Trail is to the right at about 0.75 mile. The Coppermines Trail winds to the left emerging slowly from the ravine into mixed hardwood forest, finally crossing the high point of Catfish Pond Gap at about 1.5 miles. A very gradual downhill from the gap leads to an

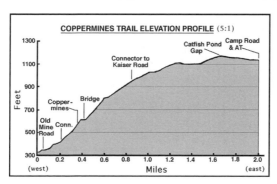

67

intersection with the AT within sight of Camp Road.

Access
The west end terminates at Old Mine Road 7.5 miles from the Water Gap. The east end terminates at the AT 50 yards west of Camp Road. There is ample parking at the Old Mine Road end and limited parking at the Camp Road end.

There are two intermediate connectors to the Kaiser Road Trail at 1/4 and 3/4 mile from Old Mine Road.

Trail Surface
Woods trail path, somewhat rocky in places and with no major wet spots. There is a foot bridge across a brook 1/2 mile from west end.

Scenery/Points of Interest
Several ancient copper mines are accessible from the trail. One is 1/2 mile east of Old Mine Road, another 0.15 mile on a spur trail which begins 100 feet from Old Mine Road. Entry into the mines is not permitted. AMC's Mohican Outdoor Center and Camp Store is 1/4 mile north of the termination and AT crossing on Camp Road. There is open hardwood forest in the eastern end and a narrow hemlock ravine with a cascading brook in the western half.

Climbing
800 feet west to east, 70 feet east to west.

Maintained by: New York-New Jersey Trail Conference.
Permitted Uses: Hiking and cross-country skiing.

Rattlesnake Swamp Trail

2.25 miles, orange blazed

General Description

This trail generally runs parallel to the AT and meets it at both ends. In addition, a short spur trail leads to the Mohican Outdoor Center near the south end of the trail.

Access to North End

There is parking for a few cars where the AT intersects NPS route 602, about 1.8 miles south of Millbrook. The AT and the Fire Tower Road are one and the same at this point. At 0.4 mile from the parking area, the AT veers off

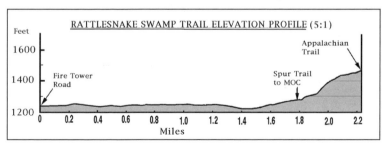

Mohican Outdoor Center Lodge

the Fire Tower Road to the left. The Fire Tower Road continues straight ahead. In another 100 yards on the Fire Tower Road, the northern end of the Rattlesnake Swamp Trail (RS) appears on the right.

Access from Mohican Outdoor Center

Take Camp Road about 1/4 mile beyond the AMC camp store to a large parking area on the left. Vehicular traffic is prohibited beyond this point. Continue on Camp Road on foot for another 1/4 mile to its end. A short sign-posted and blazed spur trail (0.15 mile) leads from the end of Camp Road to the main Rattlesnake Swamp Trail. A right turn onto the Rattlesnake Swamp Trail leads in 0.4 mile to its southern terminus at the AT. A left hand turn onto the Rattlesnake Swamp Trail will lead to the northern terminus near NPS 602.

Trail Surface

Woods trail path. It edges a swamp at the north end but there are no major wet spots. There are four easy small stream crossings in open hardwood forest in a broad valley between the swamp and the spur trail. A moderate climb on a stony path is required from the spur trail to the south end of the Rattlesnake Swamp Trail and the AT.

Scenery/Points of Interest

Distant views of Catfish Pond near the south end of the trail. A favorite loop hike is to combine the Rattlesnake Swamp Trail with the Appalachian

Trail. The AT between the Rattlesnake Swamp Trail south terminus and the Catfish Fire Tower has spectacular and continuous views of the Great Valley of the Appalachians in New Jersey.

The AMC's Mohican Outdoor Center and Camp Store is about 1/2 mile southwest of the spur trail on Camp Road. The Catfish Fire Tower on the AT is about one mile from NPS 602. If the fire tower is manned, ask for permission to climb the tower.

Climbing

From the spur trail to the northern terminus is essentially flat. From the spur trail to the southern terminus at the AT is a 320 foot climb. The reverse direction has no climbing.

Maintained By: New York-New Jersey Trail Conference.
Permitted Uses: Hiking and cross-country skiing.

AT-Camp Road to NPS 602 — *3.1 miles, white blazed*

General Description *(map on p. 69)*

Camp Road crosses the Kittatinny Range at Catfish Pond Gap on its way to the Mohican Outdoor Center. The AT crosses Camp Road, following approximately the ridge line of Kittatinny Mountain.

From Camp Road, it climbs out of the gap, 400 feet in the first 0.4 mile back to the ridge top. There is little elevation change in the next two miles as the AT follows the ridge line beyond the Catfish Fire Tower. It then descends

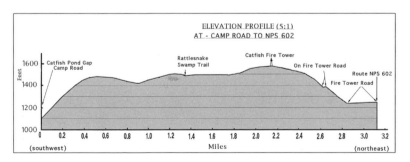

71

Daisies

300 feet into the next gap in the ridge line where NPS 602 crosses on its way to Millbrook Village.

Access

There is parking for a few cars where the AT intersects Camp Road and where it intersects NPS 602. The Rattlesnake Swamp Trail meets the AT at both ends and is a favorite loop hike when combined with the AT.

Trail Surface

It is a moderate to heavily stoned foot path except in a few places where it follows the Catfish Fire Tower Road near the NPS 602 end.

At the ridge top the woodland is sparse and scrubby because of thin soil cover over bedrock and heavy exposure to the elements. It is the highest point for many miles. Below the ridge top, a fairly mature open hardwood forest predominates.

Scenery/Points of Interest

There are continuous high and long distance views of the Great Valley from the ridge top. Because of the scrub forest and precipitous drop to the valley (about 500 feet), expansive views are available in both summer and winter.

The Catfish Fire Tower (60 feet high) is manned most of the time. Ask for permission to climb to the top. The views from the top are in all directions and quite spectacular.

Climbing

    a.) 400 feet in 0.4 mile from Camp Road to the ridge top.
    b.) 300 feet in 0.5 mile from NPS 602 to the fire tower.
    c.) Small climbs of 50 feet to 75 feet along the ridge top.

Maintained by: New York-New Jersey Trail Conference.
Permitted Uses: Hiking only.

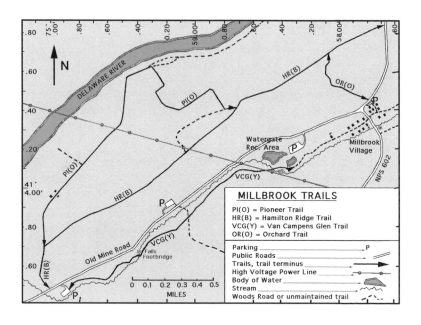

MILLBROOK TRAILS

PI(O) = Pioneer Trail
HR(B) = Hamilton Ridge Trail
VCG(Y) = Van Campens Glen Trail
OR(O) = Orchard Trail

Parking .... P
Public Roads _____
Trails, trail terminus _____▶
High Voltage Power Line _____
Body of Water _____
Stream _____
Woods Road or unmaintained trail _____

CHAPTER 5

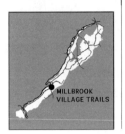

Millbrook Village Trails (DWGNRA)

• Van Campens Glen Trail / *1.65 miles*
• Orchard Trail / *0.65 mile*
• Hamilton Ridge Trail / *2.7 miles*
• Pioneer Trail / *2.2 miles*

Millbrook Village is an interesting preserved and restored 19th Century West Jersey farm village. It lies at the intersection of Old Mine Road and NPS 602. There is ample parking on Old Mine Road at a small visitor center. Most activity at the village (open houses, displays, etc.) occurs during summer weekends.

The main street of the village runs northeast to southwest. To the northeast it becomes an unmarked woods road known as Donkeys Corners Road. It intersects the paved Blue Mountain Lakes Road in about 1.5 miles. To the southwest it becomes an unmarked woods road that leads to the Watergate Recreation Area and the Van Campens Glen Trail.

The Orchard Trail begins across Old Mine Road from the northern parking area entrance. It in turn leads to the Hamilton Ridge Trail and the Pioneer Trail.

All of the trails in this section lie to the west or northwest of the AT and do not connect with it.

Van Campens Brook

Van Campens Glen Trail

1.65 miles, yellow blazed

General Description

From the southwest end the trail immediately enters a cool hemlock ravine along Van Campens Brook. The narrow trail goes up and down the sides of the ravine, crossing the brook at 0.5 mile. A series of cascades provides great scenery, culminating in a large waterfall plunging into a deep pool at its base near the stream crossing. At this point the trail begins to climb out of the ravine. It crosses Cutoff Road (parking area 200 yards to the left across Old

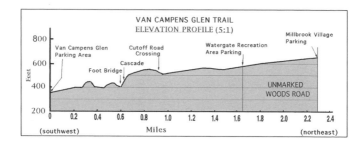

Mine Road) at 0.9 mile. From this point the trail widens slowly to a woods road ending at the Watergate Recreation Area parking lot. An unmarked woods road continues from here to Millbrook Village 0.6 mile beyond.

Access

This popular trail can be accessed at both ends from Old Mine Road, the west end at 1.9 miles west of Millbrook and the east end at 0.5 mile west of Millbrook at the Watergate Recreation Area. There is ample parking at both ends. There is also an intermediate access point at 1.2 miles west of Millbrook at the Cutoff Road parking area.

Van Campen's Glen Cascade

Trail Surface

A sometimes narrow, sometimes steep dirt path follows Van Campens Brook to the major cascade at 0.5 mile from the southeast end. A fairly smooth woods path from that point brings you to the crossing of Cutoff Road. Beyond Cutoff Road the trail follows a broad woods road.

Scenery

Van Campens Brook cascades and ravine at the southwest end of the trail are superb. The major cascade empties at 0.5 mile into a classic deep green pool of sparkling water in a natural bowl surrounded by mature forest.

Watergate Recreation Area with extensive lawns and small lakes is another area of great natural beauty.

Climbing

There are a couple of short steep climbs toward the southwest end where the trail closely follows Van Campens Brook. Other portions of the trail have gradual slopes only. The trail rises a total of 210 feet going southwest to northeast.

Maintained by: Appalachian Mountain Club.
Permitted Uses: Hiking only.

Millbrook Village

Orchard Trail   *0.65 mile, orange blazed*

General Description *(map on p. 74)*

The Orchard Trail is a pleasant wide trail through relatively recently overgrown fields. The south end starts opposite the Millbrook Village parking area off Old Mine Road (near the intersection with NPS 602). It winds gradually uphill to an old house site and spring at 0.2 mile. Near the north end the woods road traverses a mature wood lot before terminating at the Hamilton

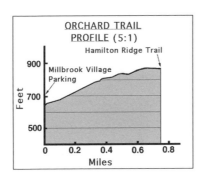

79

Ridge Road (blue blaze). A right turn on the Hamilton Ridge Road will bring you back to Old Mine Road in 0.35 mile. There is a small parking area here at 0.5 mile north of Millbrook.

Access

Use the parking area at Millbrook Village or at the Old Mine Road end of the Hamilton Ridge Trail.

Scenery/Points of Interest

Millbrook Village is a restored 19th century agricultural village. Many of the buildings are open during summer weekends.

Climbing

The trail climbs 200 feet from Millbrook Village to the Hamilton Ridge Trail.

Maintained by: New York-New Jersey Trail Conference.
Permitted Uses: Hiking, cross-country skiing.

Hamilton Ridge Trail
2.7 miles, blue blazed

General Description *(map on p. 74)*

The Hamilton Ridge Trail is an old public road which is now gated to

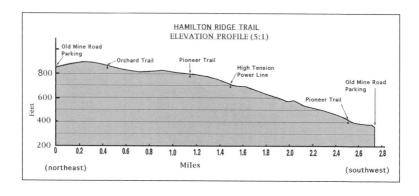

exclude motorized traffic. It begins just northeast of where Van Campens Brook crosses Old Mine Road and returns to Old Mine Road at the top of the ridge between Millbrook Village and Flatbrookville. Walking it is easy. The road is broad and relatively smooth and actually paved about halfway. Grades are light, gradually diminishing from northeast to southwest. There is evidence of several old house sites which were torn down by the DWGNRA. Portions traverse overgrown fields as well as some old open hardwood forest.

Access

There is parking for several cars at both ends of the trail off Old Mine Road. Be sure not to block the gates.

The Hamilton Ridge Trail can also be accessed from Millbrook Village via the Orchard Trail (see page 79) which intersects the Hamilton Ridge Trail about 0.35 mile from the northeast end of the trail. The Orchard Trail is 0.65 mile long.

The Pioneer Trail (see page 82) starts and ends on the Hamilton Ridge Trail also.

Scenery/Points of Interest

A pleasant and easy walk in the woods with several old house sites.

Climbing

There is a gradual elevation drop of 480 feet in 2.7 miles going from northeast to southwest.

Maintained by: New York-New Jersey Trail Conference.
Permitted Uses: Hiking, cross-country skiing.

Pioneer Trail

2.2 miles, orange blazed

General Description *(map on p. 74)*

The Pioneer Trail has been relocated to the southwest of the original trail in order to reduce human traffic at an eagle nesting site. The old trail appears on many maps. The relocated trail still begins and ends on the Hamilton Ridge Trail and follows the Delaware River for part of its length.

Starting at the northeast terminus on the Hamilton Ridge Trail (1.1 miles from Old Mine Road), the trail veers to the right on an old woods road in fairly mature forest. At 0.1 mile it turns right onto a woods path and gradually drops over a couple of low ridges in open hardwood forest. At 0.25 mile there is a sharp left turn back onto a woods road which traverses the top edge of a small ravine while dropping a bit more steeply. Where the ravine road begins to flatten, there is another sharp right onto a path at the edge of an overgrown field. At 0.75 mile it takes a left turn following an old stone row down to the cliffs above the Delaware River. We follow the river about 100 feet above it on the crest of the bluff for about 0.2 mile before going on to another woods road which veers away from the river. At 1.65 miles a newly gravelled road enters from the right and continues as the trail straight ahead. At 1.9 miles you will pass through an old farmstead where the barns and house are still standing (scheduled to be torn down). The woods road continues, rising gently from the river to the end of the trail back on the Hamilton Ridge Trail at 2.2 miles.

Access

Access to the Pioneer Trail is only via the Hamilton Ridge Trail. The northeast terminus is 1.1 miles from the northeast terminus of the Hamilton

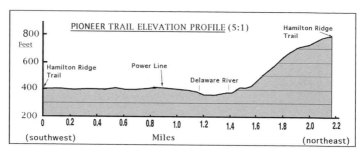

Ridge Trail at Old Mine Road. The southwest terminus is 0.2 mile from the southwest terminus of the Hamilton Ridge Trail, also at Old Mine Road. Both ends have parking for several cars.

Trail Surface

Much of the trail is woods road of varying ages. The woods roads which comprise the southwest end of the trail beyond mile 1.65 are newly gravelled.

The woods roads toward the northeast terminus before reaching the Delaware River are more ancient and partially overgrown, almost to the point where they are little more than woods paths.

None of the trail is particularly rough, stony or steep. It is an easy walking path.

Scenery/Points of Interest

The bluffs above the Delaware River are quite scenic. The trail is in hardwood forest with little or no underbrush at the top of a bluff 100 feet above the river. Views in winter months are particularly grand.

The small ravine which is encountered prior to reaching the Delaware from the northeast is also of scenic interest. The trail is about 40-70 feet above the ravine bottom in this area.

Climbing

The trail drops 400 feet from the northeast terminus to the Delaware River, sometimes fairly steeply. After leaving the Delaware traveling toward the southwest terminus, there is a gentle upward slope rising a total of 40 feet in 1.2 miles.

Maintained by: New York-New Jersey Trail Conference.
Permitted Uses: Hiking, cross-country skiing.

Buttermilk Falls

CHAPTER 6

Crater Lake Trails (DWGNRA)

- AT-NPS 602 to Blue Mountain Lakes Road / *3.85 miles*
- Crater Lake Trail / *1.65 miles*
- AT-Blue Mountain Lakes Road to Brink Road / *7.0 miles*
- Buttermilk Falls Trail / *1.6 miles*

Local mythology claims that Crater Lake was created by a meteorite sometime during the 19th century. It seems more likely this beautiful mountain feature is another glacial lake like nearby Sunfish and Catfish ponds, despite its crescent shape and the high bluffs on the northwest side.

Crater Lake is far off the beaten track. Its large parking area and picnic grounds are at the end of a 2.4 mile long gravel road (Skyline Drive) which starts at the end of Blue Mountain Lakes Road. These roads dead end 5.5 miles from Old Mine Road.

The AT crosses at the point where Blue Mountain Lakes Road turns into Skyline Drive.

Buttermilk Falls is the highest falls in New Jersey, about 200 feet high. It is best viewed in spring since at other seasons the water volume is quite low. The falls are at the western end of the Buttermilk Falls Trail, which is several miles from Walpack on the gravel Mountain Road.

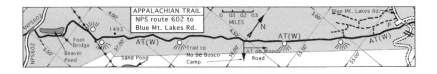

AT-NPS 602 to Blue Mountain Lakes Road

3.85 miles, white blazed

General Description

This portion of the AT closely follows the Kittatinny Ridge top for over three miles. There is little climbing other than the ascent to the top of the ridge about 0.5 mile from NPS 602. The ridge here is bordered on the east by a 300 to 400 foot steep escarpment, providing continuous views of the Great Valley, especially in winter. The second half (2.2 to 3.85 miles from NPS 602) follows a wide and almost flat woods road that was once part of a housing development since eliminated by the NPS.

There is a marked trail leading to the Northern New Jersey Council, Boy Scouts of America, No Be Bosco camp to the right at 1.55 miles from NPS 602. Access to the camp is by permission from the council.

Access

There is parking for several cars where the AT intersects NPS 602. The AT at this point follows NPS 602 south for about 0.1 mile before turning right into the woods. See the description of the AT segment from Camp Road to NPS 602. At the north end at Blue Mountain Lakes Road, there is a moderate sized parking area just west of where the AT intersects the road. The AT at this

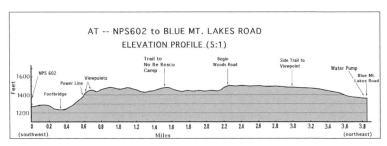

Field of flowers

point goes right onto Blue Mountain Lakes Road for only 100 feet before it re-enters the woods to the left. There is a potable water pump between the parking area and the trail just south of Blue Mountain Lakes Road.

Trail Surface

At the NPS 602 end, the trail starts on a broad smooth woods road. After about 0.1 mile the trail turns left off the road onto a woods path in a mature forest. Between 0.3 to 0.4 mile from NPS 602 there may be some wet spots associated with a pond recently created by beavers.

From 0.4 to 0.7 mile from NPS 602 the woods path climbs to the top of the Kittatinny Ridge, crossing under an overhead powerline in the process.

From 0.7 mile to 2.2 miles the AT remains a typical moderately stony woods path. At 2.2 miles it joins a smooth broad woods road which was once part of a housing development. It follows this road all the way to Blue Mountain Lakes Road.

Scenery/Points of Interest

There are specific viewpoints at 0.65 to 0.7 mile where the trail first tops the ridge, and at 3.0 miles where a short side trail heads to a view over Fairview Lake. But the trail continuously borders a sharp 300 to 400 foot escarpment providing views over the Great Valley from 0.7 mile to about 3.6 miles.

Climbing

There is only one significant climb of 230 feet from just beyond the beaver pond at 0.55 mile to the ridge top at 0.7 mile. At the north end the trail gradually descends about 140 feet to Blue Mountain Lakes Road.

Maintained by: New York-New Jersey Trail Conference.
Permitted Uses: Hiking only.

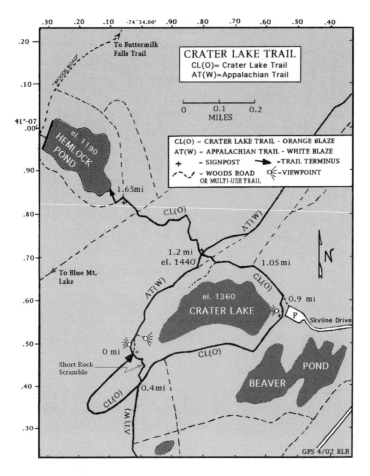

CRATER LAKE TRAIL
CL(O)= Crater Lake Trail
AT(W)=Appalachian Trail

0   0.1   0.2
MILES

CL(O) = CRATER LAKE TRAIL - ORANGE BLAZE
AT(W) = APPALACHIAN TRAIL - WHITE BLAZE
+ = SIGNPOST   = TRAIL TERMINUS
= WOODS ROAD   = VIEWPOINT
OR MULTI-USE TRAIL

GPS 4/02 RLB

Crater Lake Trail

1.65 miles, orange blazed

General Description

The Crater Lake Trail starts at the AT just west of Crater Lake. It winds to the west down a gradual grade on woods roads to cross the AT at 0.4 mile. It then follows the south shore of Crater Lake to the parking area (0.9 mile) at the end of Skyline Drive. There is an impressive view of the lake at this point. Follow the trail northward as it winds through a small picnic area onto a graveled road which leads to the local fire monitoring station. The trail leaves the gravel road and turns left back onto woods roads at 1.05 miles. Follow the blazes uphill and cross the AT again at 1.2 miles. You are 80 feet above the lake at this point. The trail then winds downhill through hemlock and laurel to the shores of Hemlock Pond at 1.65 miles.

By turning left onto the AT at the second crossing (1.2 miles) the starting point is reached in 0.3 mile for a total round trip of 1.5 miles. Another excellent view of the lake is available off the AT just prior to the Crater Lake Trail starting point. This loop hike around Crater Lake combining the Crater Lake Trail and the AT can also be started at the Crater Lake parking area, of course.

You can connect to the "Woods Road" trail by taking the last woods road around Hemlock Pond to the right or the left. Or you can reverse course back to the ridge above Crater Lake and either follow the AT back to the Crater Lake terminus or follow the Crater Lake Trail back to the parking lot.

Access from the Crater Lake Parking Area

The trail can be accessed either from the AT or from the parking lot at the end of Skyline Drive which is a gravel extension of the Blue Mountain Lakes Road.

Trail Surface

Most of the trail follows old woods roads, so the path is mostly smooth and broad. The exception is between the north AT crossing and Hemlock

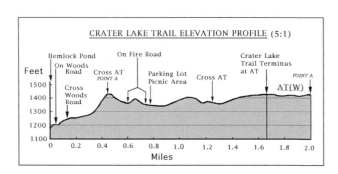

Crater Lake

Pond which is a typical steep and stony woods path.

Scenery/Points of Interest

Crater Lake is a beautiful high elevation Kittatinny lake. It has a small beach near the parking area and interesting bluffs above the lake on the west side. Views of the lake are available from several points on the trail. Hemlock Pond is a beautiful and isolated man-made lake.

Climbing

Most climbing on this trail is between Hemlock Pond and the AT crossing north of the lake, about 250 feet. A small amount of climbing (80 feet) is also required between the parking lot and the same AT crossing.

Maintained By: New York -New Jersey Trail Conference.
Permitted Uses: Hiking and cross-country skiing.

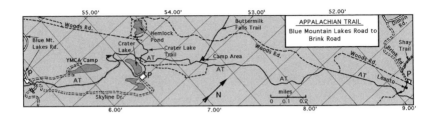

AT-Blue Mountain Lakes Road to Brink Road

7.0 miles, white blazed

General Description

This section of the AT continues to follow the top of the Kittatinny Ridge, providing views in two directions, toward Pennsylvania and toward the Great Valley in New Jersey. The terrain is nevertheless quite varied, traversing the north side of Crater Lake and peaking at Rattlesnake Mountain and Bird Mountain prior to dropping down to Brink Road to a elevation of 1150 feet at the northeast end.

Access

There are parking areas where the AT crosses the paved Blue Mountain Lakes Road. Just beyond the AT crossing, the road ends at a barrier. Gravel surfaced Skyline Drive continues to the left and dead ends in a large parking area at Crater Lake in 2.3 miles.

The AT can also be accessed from the Crater Lake parking area by following the new Crater Lake Trail (orange blazed) for a quarter mile in either direction

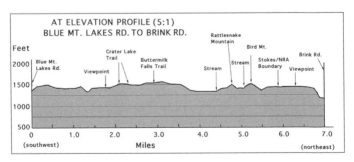

Hemlock Pond

from the parking area. The Crater Lake Trail, which incorporates the old Hemlock Pond Trail, starts at the AT (1.7 miles from Blue Mountain Lakes Road) and immediately turns back, recrossing the AT at 1.6 miles from Blue Mountain Lakes Road. It then loops around the south and northeast sides of the lake, crossing the AT again at 2.1 miles from its starting point, then dropping down to Hemlock Pond.

About 0.75 mile beyond the last Crater Lake Trail crossing, the AT encounters the Buttermilk Falls Trail (blue blazed), the other end of which is 1.6 miles and a 1100 foot drop away at Mountain Road. A camping area just off the AT is available here.

Access is also available at Brink Road. A small parking area is available where Brink Road crosses Woods Road about 0.2 mile north of the AT along the Shay Trail which follows the old road bed (brown over yellow blazed). Both Brink and Shay Roads are high-clearance 4WD driveable only.

Trail Surface

The AT follows old woods road beds from the start of the Crater Lake Trail to just beyond the Buttermilk Falls Trail. Another woods road section is at Bird Mountain where it follows the bed of the track known as "Woods Road" for about 0.5 mile.

All other parts of the trail are stony woods paths. There is a short rock scramble between where the Crater Lake Trail first crosses the AT and where the same trail begins 0.1 mile beyond. In this immediate area is the Harding Lake Rock Shelter, a prehistoric site (cave) which was excavated in the 1940s. Human occupation was indicated starting more than 5000 years ago.

Small stream crossings are necessary both before and after ascending Rattlesnake Mountain at 4.4 and 5.1 miles from Blue Mountain Lakes Road.

Scenery/Points of Interest

Starting from Blue Mountain Road, the first overlook just past the trailhead of the Crater Lake Trail provides views of the Delaware Valley and the Pocono Plateau in Pennsylvania. At the top of Rattlesnake Mountain (4.8 miles) and Bird Mountain (5.6 miles) and halfway between Bird Mountain and Brink Road (6.3 miles), northwest views are also available.

The trail is in mostly open mixed hardwood forest, but at the higher elevations there are areas of scrub growth and just plain bare rock.

The Harding Lake Rock Shelter, a pre-historic site excavated in the 1940s, is 1.65 miles from Blue Mountain Lakes Road. It may be hard to find.

Climbing

From Blue Mountain Lakes Road to Brink Road:

 a. 150 feet just beyond Blue Mountain Lakes Road
 b. small rock scramble at 1.65 miles
 c. 200 feet to Rattlesnake Mountain
 d. 150 feet to Bird Mountain

From Brink Road to Blue Mountain Lakes Road:

 a. 250 feet just southwest of Brink Road
 b. 200 feet to Bird Mountain
 c.)150 feet to Rattlesnake Mountain
 d. 300 feet to ending at Buttermilk Falls Trail

Maintained by: New York-New Jersey Trail Conference.
Permitted Uses: Hiking only.

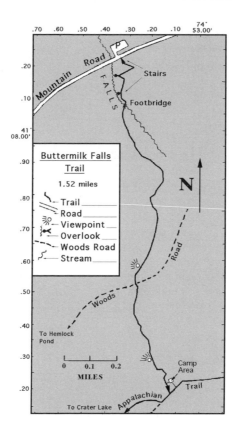

Buttermilk Falls Trail

1.6 miles, blue blazed

General Description

Buttermilk Falls is the highest waterfall in New Jersey. The creek cascades in several stages dropping over 200 feet at the north end of the trail just south of Mountain Road. There is a parking area off Mountain Road opposite the falls.

The trail rises steeply for the first 0.25-mile from Mountain Road skirting the cascade on wood and stone steps and boardwalks. Once above the falls the trail crosses the stream and steeply climbs the ravine on the opposite side. A more gradual but steady upslope in hardwood forest continues to the end point at the AT. The trail crosses the Woods Road Trail (unblazed) at about 0.8 mile from Mountain Road. An AT camping area is on the left just before reaching the AT.

Access

Mountain Road is best reached by turning off Old Mine Road to go through the middle of Walpack Center Village. This becomes Brink Road. At 0.5 mile east of the village, beyond the cemetery, Brink Road crosses a dirt road. This is Mountain Road. Turn right to reach the Buttermilk Falls parking lot in 2.0 miles.

Trail Surface

At the Mountain Road end, the trail is wood steps and gravel from the road to above the falls. A woods path in open forest climbs steeply out of the ravine south of the falls. The remainder of the trail is a moderately stony woods path.

Scenery/Points of Interest

Buttermilk Falls during a wet season is worth a journey.

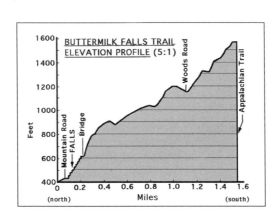

96

Climbing

The Mountain Road end of the trail has stairways and slopes in excess of 20% grade for short stretches. Total climbing from Mountain Road to the AT is about 1100 feet.

Maintained by: New York-New Jersey Trail Conference.
Permitted Uses: Hiking trail only.

Van Campen Inn

CHAPTER 7

Walpack Center Trails (DWGNRA)

• Walpack Ridge Trail / *2.55 miles*
• Military Road Trail / *1.15 miles*
• Tillman's Ravine Trails / *0.95 mile*

T he preserved farming village of Walpack Center is a bit smaller than Millbrook and was more recently occupied. It has a post office, church, firehouse, cemetery, and a few houses. The post office has a small parking area at the junction of NPS 615 and the main street of the village. Beyond the village the main street becomes Brink Road, which is gated (closed) in winter (December to April) and used as a cross-country ski trail. The Military Road Trail and Walpack Ridge Trail start across NPS 615 from the post office. The Tillman's Ravine Trail is included here because of its proximity to the village on Brink Road, even though it is in Stokes State Forest. Walpack Center village is part of the Delaware Water Gap National Recreation Area.

None of these trails connects to the AT or the main Kittatinny ridge line.

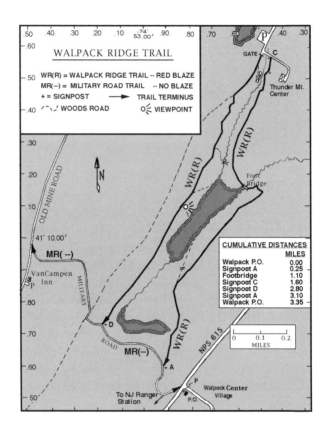

Walpack Ridge Trail

2.55 miles, red blazed

General Description

This trail begins and ends at Military Road, 0.25 and 0.55 mile from the Walpack Center post office off NPS 615. Military Road is a woods road which connects Walpack Center to the Van Campen Inn on Old Mine Road. There is a small parking area at the Walpack post office, where Military Road begins. Red blazes for the Walpack Ridge Trail have been added here, but the actual start of the trail is 1/4 mile beyond. A signpost at that point marks the trail entrance to the right.

The trail traverses gentle slopes in open hardwood forest along a ridge skirting a large beaver pond on the left. At 0.35 mile an old path leads down to the beaver pond and at 0.8 mile the trail switchbacks down the side of the ridge to cross a creek on a foot bridge (0.9 mile).

Across the bridge is low lying open hardwood followed by an overgrown field before the trail emerges at the Thunder Mountain Educational Center. Follow the trail below the Center to a driveway. Another signpost here directs you to the left down the driveway for about 100 yards where the continuation of the Walpack Ridge Trail leaves on an old woods road to the left. It follows the woods road for 0.2 mile before turning left down a gentle slope in a relatively young forest. After another 1/4-mile good views of the beaver pond appear on the left. The trail soon reaches Military Road, where you can turn left and walk back to the village and your car.

Access

The Walpack Ridge Trail begins and ends on Military Road (sometimes

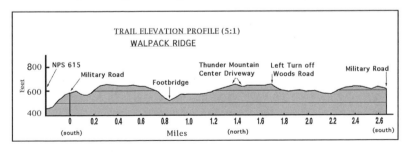

101

called Military Highway). Best access is from the small parking area at the Walpack post office on NPS 615, which is directly opposite the Military Road Trail terminus. Since the Military Road Trail is not blazed, blazes for the Walpack Ridge Trail have been added at this point. The actual Walpack Ridge Trail terminates at Military Road 0.25 mile from NPS 615.

Trail Surface

For most of its length it is a quite smooth forest path with few rocks. In the vicinity of the Thunder Mountain Center it is a woods road or field edge or driveways, all of which are broad, smooth and easy to walk.

Scenery/Points of Interest

The beaver pond has a great deal of evidence of beaver activity. Walpack Center is a small historic community which is being preserved by the NPS. There are no current residents other than park personnel. Van Campen Inn, at the end of Military Road, is a preserved colonial stone building open to the public, but only during special events.

Climbing

Slopes are very gentle other than the beginning of Military Road at NPS 615 and the switchback down the slope to the footbridge crossing at the Northeast end of the beaver pond.

Maintained by: New York-New Jersey Trail Conference
Permitted Uses: Hiking, cross-country skiing.

Military Road Trail   *1.15 miles, unblazed*

General Description *(map on p. 100)*

Sometimes also called Military Highway, this trail is a woods road between Walpack Center village and the Van Campen Inn on Old Mine Road. It also serves as the access to the Walpack Ridge Trail (see above). The Military Road is not blazed, but blazes for the Walpack Ridge Trail have been added at the Walpack Center village end of the trail, although the Walpack Ridge Trail "officially" starts a quarter mile to the west. Both terminations of the Walpack Ridge Trail on Military Road are signed and blazed.

Access

Military Road can be accessed from NPS 615 at Walpack Center village. Parking for a few cars is available at the old village post office at the corner of NPS 615 and the main street of the village (Brink Road). The west end of the trail on Old Mine Road is about 0.1 mile from the Van Campen Inn which also has parking for a few cars.

The trail can be accessed via the Walpack Ridge Trail at 0.2 and 0.5 mile from the eastern end.

Trail Surface

A broad woods road with some erosion at steep parts exists for the entire length of the trail. It is gated to prevent motorized traffic.

Scenery/Points of Interest

Walpack Center village, now essentially abandoned, is being preserved due to its historic value. Van Campen Inn, a classic colonial style stone building, is also being preserved by the National Park Service.

Climbing

From Walpack Center, the trail goes up moderately steeply at the start, climbing a total of almost 150 feet to the first trailhead of the Walpack Ridge

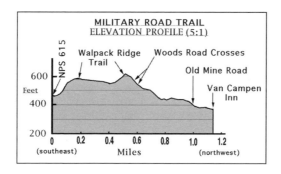

Walpack Center Village

Trail. It drops back down 200 feet before ending at Old Mine Road.

Maintained by: Appalachian Mountain Club.
Permitted Uses: Hiking.

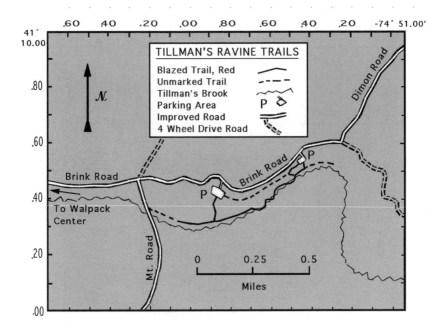

Tillman's Ravine Trails

0.95 mile, red diamond blazed

General Description

East of Walpack Center village, paralleling Brink Road, lies Tillman's Ravine. From two parking areas the trail descends into the ravine and follows the brook down to Mountain Road. In the ravine the trails crisscross the brook many times on plank footbridges between steep walls and cascades, allowing a close familiarity with a small, cascading mountain stream.

Access

There are two parking areas on the right side of Brink Road. The lower one is about one mile from Walpack Center and the upper one about 1.5 miles.

Trails descend from both parking areas into the ravine less than 1/4 mile to the south of the road. The upper parking area has two blazed alternative routes to the stream. The elevation profile shows only the shortest route. The

Tillman's Ravine Trail

spur trail from the lower parking area to the stream is also shown on the elevation profile. A right turn where this spur meets the main trail will bring you to gravel surfaced Mountain Road. This part of the trail is not blazed the entire way, however.

The most interesting portion of the trail lies in the ravine between the two parking areas.

Trail Surface

The spur trails from the parking areas are well traveled with moderate grades and few stones. The trail in the ravine has several bridges and boardwalks over and around the stream. A major portion is on top of large, relatively flat, rocks.

Scenery/Points of Interest

The trail through the ravine allows an intimate familiarity with a beautiful small, cascading mountain stream.

Climbing

Total elevation change from the upper parking area to Mountain Road is 350 feet.

Maintained by: New York-New Jersey Trail Conference.
Permitted Uses: Hiking only.

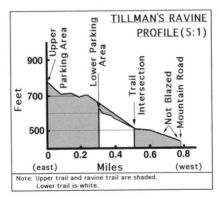

The Steffen Trail in a Pine Plantation

CHAPTER 8

Stokes State Forest Southwest Trails (SSF)

- Stoll Trail / *0.65 mile*
- Shay Trail / *1.4 miles*
- Steffen Trail / *1.75 miles*
- Ladder Trail / *0.45 mile*
- AT-Brink Road to Culver Tower / *5.5 miles*
- Acropolis Trail / *0.55 mile*

All Stokes State Forest trails to the south and west of U.S. 206, with the exception of the Tillman's Ravine Trails, are described here.

The Stoll Trail is a pretty, short and fairly level trail also good for cross-country skiing in winter.

The Shay Trail is contiguous with Shay Road and Brink Road, both of which are open to vehicular traffic except in winter, when the gates are locked for cross-country skiing.

The Steffen, Jacob's Ladder and the Acropolis trails, along with part of the AT, form a loop around Kittatinny Lake. The loop begins and ends on U.S. 206.

Because much of the nearby land is private, these trails remain relatively isolated.

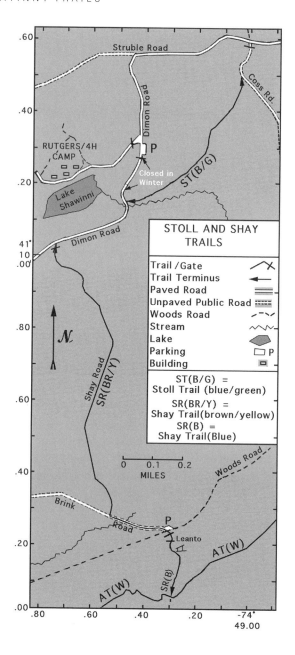

Stoll Trail
0.65 mile, blue over green blazed

General Description

The Stoll Trail is a pretty little trail which begins in a small ravine at the Dimon Road end. It climbs gradually out of the ravine away from the brook on a smooth woods path ending at Coss Road in fairly mature forest. A left turn on Coss Road brings you to Struble Road in 0.2 mile, for a total of 0.75 mile.

Access

There is a large parking area opposite the entrance to the Rutgers/4H Camp on Dimon Road, about 0.25 mile from the Stoll trailhead. In winter Dimon Road is closed (gated and not snow plowed) beyond this point.

There is parking for about two cars at the junction of Coss Road, a gated park road, and Struble Road, a paved public road.

Trail Surface

Fairly smooth woods path. Coss Road is four-wheel drive-able if the gate is open.

Climbing

A very gradual 100-foot climb from Dimon Road to Struble Road.

Maintained by: New York-New Jersey Trail Conference
Permitted Uses: Hiking, hunting, horseback riding, bicycling, snowmobiling, cross-country skiing.

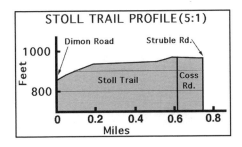

Shay Trail

1.4 miles, brown over yellow blazed, north end

blue blazed, south end

General Description

Shay Trail follows Shay Road starting at Dimon Road (paved) and ending at Brink Road. It then turns left onto Brink Road (at 1.0 mile), crosses Woods Road (1.2 miles) and terminates at the AT (1.4 miles). Both Shay and Brink Roads are rough dirt roads with major amounts of erosion. They are open to vehicular traffic from April to November, but are best negotiated with a high clearance four-wheel drive vehicle. In winter the gates at the bottom of both roads are closed to accommodate cross-country skiing and snowmobiling. Brink Road just beyond Woods Road is permanently blocked to vehicles with a double row of large boulders.

Shay Trail hardly deserves description as a trail, but it is blazed brown over yellow at the lower north end of Shay Road and blazed blue between the leanto and the AT at the upper southern end. In between the blazes seem to lapse, but there is no problem in following the roads.

Access

A few cars can be parked at the lower north end just off Dimon Road. there is also a small parking area where Brink Road crosses Woods Road.

Trail Surface

The trail surface the entire way is a rough dirt road with significant erosion in many locations.

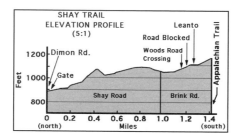

Climbing

From Dimon Road to the AT is a total climb of about 250 feet. There are a few moderately steep sections but it is mostly gradual.

Maintained by: New Jersey Forest Service
Permitted Uses: Hiking, cross-country skiing, hunting, horseback riding, bicycling, snowmobiling.

Steffen Trail   *1.75 miles, black over gray blazed*

General Description

A trail designed specifically for cross-country skiing, the Steffen Trail is also a pleasant warmer season hiking trail. Starting on Struble Road just 700 feet from U.S. 206, the trail climbs very gradually through a beautiful old pine tree plantation and then emerges into relatively mature hardwood forest. At 0.65 mile the trail merges with a woods road and turns right. A gradual descent continuing on the woods road to Coss Road begins at about 1.3 miles. The trail ends at Coss Road at 1.75 miles.

Access

There is a large parking area almost opposite the trailhead on Struble Road. This car park is also apparently used to store road materials by the State Forest workers.

There is parking for a few cars where Coss Road intersects Woods Road about 0.1 mile beyond the end of the trail. Coss Road is an unimproved

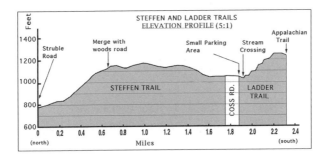

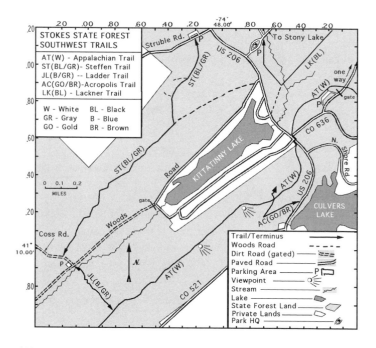

gravel/dirt road which is open from early April to mid-December. In the winter months it is gated and acts as a cross-country ski trail.

Trail Surface

The woods path from Struble Road to the junction with the woods road has been made broad and relatively stone free to accommodate cross-country skiing. The woods road portion is typically broad and smooth as well.

Climbing

A gradual 390 foot climb to about 1.0 mile, followed by a gradual descent of 120 feet to Coss Road at 1.75 miles.

Maintained by: New York-New Jersey Trail Conference.
Permitted Uses: Hiking, hunting, horseback riding, bicycling, snowmobiling, cross-country skiing.

114

Ladder Trail

Ladder Trail *0.45 mile, blue over gray blazed*

General Description

Also known as Jacob's Ladder Trail, this is a short (0.45 mile) connector between the end of Coss Road where it meets Woods Road and the AT. It rises 240 feet in a series of steps to the AT, after first crossing the small brook which is the main feed stream to Kittatinny Lake.

Access

A small parking area exists at the junction of Coss Road and Woods Road. These roads are best negotiated with 4WD vehicles and are open only early April to mid-December. Their gates are locked during the winter months.

The upper end of the trail is at the AT several miles from the nearest parking area.

Trail Surface

The trail is a moderately stony woods path for its entire length. Alternating

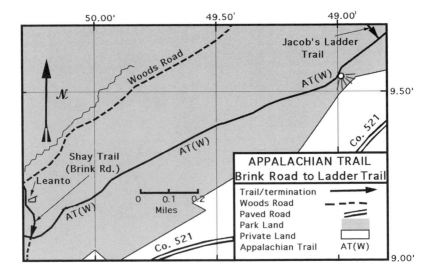

steep and gradual trail sections of several hundred feet long create a step-wise rise in elevation, in some short sections almost requiring a scramble.

Scenery

The area surrounding the lower end of the trail at Woods Road with a pleasant stream crossing is quite scenic. If the AT is taken to the NE after the upper end of the trail is reached, several excellent views of Lake Owasa and Culvers Lake emerge.

Climbing

A step-wise climb of 240 feet in 0.45 mile has an average slope of 10% (see elevation profile on page 113).

Maintained by: New York-New Jersey Trail Conference.
Permitted Uses: Hiking, cross-country skiing.

AT-Brink Road to Culver Tower   *5.5 miles, white blazed*

General Description (maps on pp. 114, 116)

The AT continues to closely follow the top of the Kittatinny Ridge, which is quite distinct in this section and at 1,300 feet to 1,400 foot elevation.

Starting at the small gap at Brink Road, the trail quickly climbs to the top of the ridge. It dips again, just 110 feet to where the Ladder Trail terminates on the left at 1.6 miles from Brink Road. There are good viewpoints along this section of trail, particularly at 1.4, 2.1 and 2.7 miles from Brink Road.

After the last viewpoint, the trail turns sharply right and descends, rather steeply at first, to the Acropolis Trail crossing at 3.0 miles. It continues to descend along the eastern flank of the Kittatinny ridge down to Culvers Gap at 935 feet where it first crosses U.S. 206, turns left and immediately crosses County Road 636 (Upper North Shore Road).

Two-tenths of a mile beyond at 3.8 miles the trail skirts a major parking area just off Sunrise Mountain Road. It crosses Sunrise Mountain Road at 4.0 miles and ascends back up the ridge, which reaches 1,515 feet at the Culver Fire Tower (formerly known as the Normanook Tower). A few hundred feet beyond the fire tower the Tower Trail descends to the left.

Access

At the Brink Road end of the trail there is a small parking area about a quarter mile west of the AT where Brink Road intersects Woods Road (see Shay Trail). Brink Road is blue blazed here to direct the through hiker to a leanto shelter about 0.15 mile west of the AT.

There is also a small parking area off Coss Road where it intersects Woods Road (see Steffen and Ladder Trails). The Ladder Trail can be taken from this parking area 0.5 mile east to the AT.

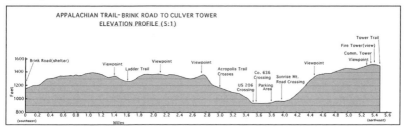

Culvers Gap

Best access is from the Culvers Gap parking area just off Sunrise Mountain Road about 0.3 mile from U.S. 206. Turn off U.S. 206 onto County Road 636 (Upper North Shore Road) and turn left in 0.25 mile onto Sunrise Mountain Road followed by a final immediate left into the parking area.

One can also access this trail via the Tower Trail which begins at the Stony Lake Trail hub (see Chapter 10) and crosses Sunrise Mountain Road 0.4 mile to the north of the AT at the Culver Fire Tower.

Trail Surface

Between Brink Road and the last viewpoint before the Acropolis Trail, it is a moderately stony woods path in open hardwood which tends to become scrubby at the ridge top.

From this viewpoint to the U.S. 206 crossing, the trail is on a broad and fairly smooth woods trail.

From U.S. 206 to the Sunrise Mountain Road crossing there is a smooth, lightly stoned woods path which becomes moderately to heavily stoned beyond.

Scenery/Points of Interest

The viewpoints in all directions on this trail section are outstanding and frequent. It is perhaps the best section of the AT in New Jersey for long distance viewing. The close proximity of lakes Owassa, Kittatinny and Stony adds considerably to the magnificence of the views.

The Culver Fire Tower can be climbed if it is manned and you can obtain permission. But it is hardly necessary as the ground views are so spectacular.

Climbing

Ascents:

a. from Brink Road to the ridge top, 220 feet
b. from Sunrise Mountain Road to Culver Fire Tower, 580 feet
c. from Ladder Trail to ridge top, 100 feet

Descents:

a. from ridge top to Ladder Trail, 150 feet
b. from ridge top to U.S. 206, 450 feet

Maintained by: New York-New Jersey Trail Conference.
Permitted Uses: Hiking only.

Acropolis Trail
0.55 mile, gold over brown blazed

General Description *(map on p. 114)*

A short connecting trail between U.S. 206 and the AT, the Acropolis is among the steepest trails in Stokes State Forest.

The wide smooth woods road trail surface makes negotiating the trail relatively easy, however.

Access

There is no parking at the lower U.S. 206 end of the trail. Cars can usually be parked at several commercial establishments just a short distance to the east on U.S. 206.

The upper end of the trail crosses the AT at 0.5 mile from U.S. 206 and peters out a short distance beyond. If you take the AT to the right (northeast), you will encounter U.S. 206 again in 0.45 mile.

Trail Surface

Broad, smooth woods road for its entire length.

Scenery

Continuous views to the right of Culvers Lake and U.S. 206 in winter months.

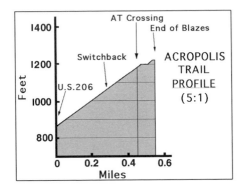

Culvers Lake

Climbing

A smooth, constant ascent of 310 feet in 0.55 mile for an average grade of eleven percent.

Maintained by: New York-New Jersey Trail Conference.
Permitted Uses: Hiking, cross-country skiing.

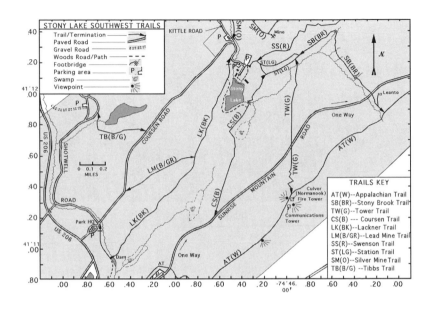

STONY LAKE SOUTHWEST TRAILS

Trail/Termination	
Paved Road	
Gravel Road	
Woods Road/Path	
Footbridge	
Parking area	P
Swamp	
Viewpoint	

KITTLE ROAD

SM(O)

SM(O) Mine

SS(R)

SB(BR)

SB(BR)

N

P

ST(LG)

ST(LG)

Leanto

Stony
Lake

TW(G)

One Way

P

COURSEN ROAD

LK(BK)

CS(B)

TB(B/G)

TW(G) ROAD

AT(W)

0   0.1   0.2
MILES

LM(B/GR)

CS(B)

MOUNTAIN

US 206

SHOTWELL

SUNRISE

Culver
(Normanook)
Fire Tower

ROAD

LK(BK)

Communications
Tower

US 206

Park HQ

41°11
.00

Dam

AT

One Way

AT(W)

TRAILS KEY

AT(W)--Appalachian Trail
SB(BR)--Stony Brook Trail
TW(G)--Tower Trail
CS(B) --- Coursen Trail
LK(BK)--Lackner Trail
LM(B/GR)--Lead Mine Trail
SS(R)--Swenson Trail
ST(LG)--Station Trail
SM(O)--Silver Mine Trail
TB(B/G) --Tibbs Trail

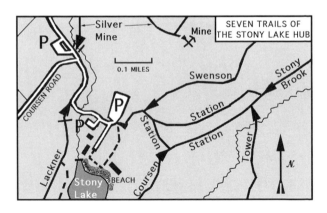

SEVEN TRAILS OF
THE STONY LAKE HUB

Silver
Mine

Mine

P

0.1 MILES

Swenson

Stony
Brook

COURSEN ROAD

P

Station

Station

P

Station

Lackner

Tower

Stony
Lake

BEACH

Coursen

N

CHAPTER 9

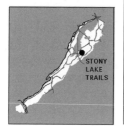

Stony Lake Trails Southwest (SSF)

- Station Trail / *0.45 mile*
- Coursen Trail / *1.2 miles*
- Tower Trail / *1.45 miles*
- Stony Brook Trail / *1.45 miles*
- Lackner Trail / *2.2 miles*
- Lead Mine Trail / *0.6 mile*
- Tibbs Trail / *0.5 mile*

The Stony Lake Day Use Area is a major trail hub of the Stokes State Forest. Seven trails terminate here, going to virtually every point on the compass.

The Stony Brook and Tower Trails can be taken south to the AT which continues to follow the top of the Kittatinny ridge line here. The Coursen Trail goes to Sunrise Mountain Road, the Lackner Trail to the Park Headquarters near U.S. 206 and the Silver Mine Trail goes almost to Skellinger Road and the State School of Conservation. The Swenson Trail goes northeast to end near Steam Mill Campground.

The Station Trail is a short loop connector trail which provides access to the Swenson, Stony Brook, Tower and Coursen trails from the main day use area parking lot. The day use area around Stony Lake has a swimming beach, picnic area, pavilion and playground.

This section covers the trails on the south and west side of the Stony Lake hub. The following section covers trails to the north and east of the hub.

Station Trail

0.8 mile, light green blazed

General Description *(map on p. 122)*

A short, wide, smooth loop trail, the Station Trail serves as a connector to four other trails which terminate in the vicinity of the Stony Lake Day Use Area: the Swenson, Coursen, Stony Brook and Tower trails.

Note that the blazing of the four trails that connect to the Station Trail continues to the large Stony Lake parking area beyond the termination points shown on the maps in this section. The sign board at the parking area, however, says "Station Trail" and mentions no others. I have chosen to follow the sign board rather than the blazes in the interest of not describing the same half-mile of trail five times. One can, however, follow the blaze marks of any of the five trails—Station, Swenson, Stony Brook, Tower or Coursen, starting at the main parking area.

Access

Main access is from the large parking area for the Stony Lake Day Use Area. The trail starts on the south end of the lot.

Trail Surface

A wide, almost stone-free woods road for its entire length.

Climbing

There is a moderate 50-foot climb from the parking area to just beyond

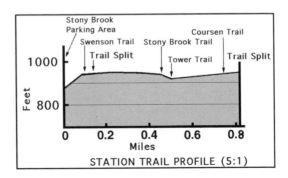

the intersection with the Swenson Trail at 0.1 mile (10% grade).

Maintained by: New York-New Jersey Trail Conference
Permitted Uses: Hiking, cross-country skiing, hunting, horseback riding, bicycling,

Coursen Trail

1.2 miles, blue blazed

General Description *(map on p. 122)*

The Coursen Trail is one of the four trails which terminate on the Station Trail, but the trail blazes continue on the Station Trail to the Stony Lake Day Use Area parking lot. Pick up the Coursen Trail (blue) blazes just beyond the "Station Trail" signpost at the west end of the parking area. In 0.1 mile the Station Trail forks and the Coursen Trail blazes take the right fork. In another 300 feet the Coursen Trail leaves the Station Trail to the right. This description covers the Coursen Trail from this point to its other termination at Sunrise Mountain Road 1.2 miles to the southwest.

At 0.2 mile from the intersection with the Station Trail, the Coursen Trail crosses Stony Brook on a foot bridge. Stony Lake can be seen in the distance to the right shortly after the stream crossing. An unnamed and unmaintained light green blazed trail, which circles Stony Lake on the southwest side and terminates on the Lackner Trail, leaves to the right at 0.4 mile. From this point the trail rises with some wet spots and then descends gradually to terminate on Sunrise Mountain Road.

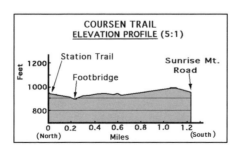

Stony Lake Beach

Access

The trail begins (but the blazes don't) at 0.15 mile from the Stony Lake Day Use parking area on the Station Trail. The Tower, Stony Brook and Swenson trails also terminate on the short loop Station Trail, so it is easy to access any of these trails from the Coursen Trail. The southwest termination is on Sunrise Mountain Road. This trail does not cross the road and continue on to the AT, unlike the Tower and Stony Brook trails. You can park anywhere on the right side of the one-way Sunrise Mountain Road.

Trail Surface

From the Station Trail to Stony Brook and a bit beyond the trail follows old woods roads which are quite broad and smooth. Beyond up to Sunrise

Mountain Road, it is an easy to negotiate lightly to moderately stoned woods path.

Scenery/Points of Interest

Stony Lake, easily accessed from the Coursen Trail, has a beach, picnic area, rest rooms and pavilion. The lake is another pretty, high glacial lake, typical of the Kittatinny Ridge. The trail traverses chiefly open hardwood forest.

Climbing

There is a gentle up slope of less than 100 feet going south-southwest from Stony Brook. The high point is about 0.1 mile from Sunrise Mountain Road and the path descends gently from that point to the road.

Maintained by: New York-New Jersey Trail Conference.
Permitted Uses: Hiking, cross-country skiing, hunting, horseback riding, bicycling, snowmobiling.

Tower Trail   *1.45 miles, green blazed*

General Description *(map on p. 122)*

The northern end of the Tower Trail is at the Station Trail, just west of where the Station Trail intersects the Stony Brook Trail. If you park at the Stony Brook Day Use parking area, take the Station Trail at the west end of the

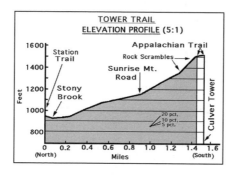

parking area. Take the left fork where the Station Trail splits at 0.15 mile. Turn right, continuing to follow the light green blazed Station Trail where it meets the Stony Brook Trail. The beginning of the Tower Trail is on the left in about 100 yards. In another 100 yards, the Tower Trail crosses Stony Brook. There is no bridge and the crossing can be a bit difficult in high water.

After the brook the trail ascends very gradually at first, slowly increasing in slope up to Sunrise Mountain Road at 0.9 mile.

Beyond Sunrise Mountain Road, the slope continues to steepen, getting to over 20% just prior to terminating at the AT at 1.45 miles. The Culver (formerly Normanook) Fire Tower is about 200 feet to the right of this trail intersection. A communications tower is just beyond.

The Tower Trail runs almost perfectly north/south.

Access

The trail can be accessed from the Stony Brook Day Use Area as described above with about 0.5 mile of walking on the Station Trail. Note that the Tower Trail blazes show the trail beginning at the Stony Lake parking area and the Tower Trail blazes can be followed from that point. The trail signpost does not indicate the Tower Trail beginning.

Parking is also allowed on the right shoulder of Sunrise Mountain Road where the Tower Trail crosses. The road is one-way (southwest to northeast) at this point.

Trail Surface

Between the Stony Brook crossing and Sunrise Mountain Road, the path is generally moderately stony and very straight in open hardwood and hemlock forest.

Beyond Sunrise Mountain Road the path becomes heavily stoned. The last tenth of a mile before terminating at the AT is quite steep, requiring rock scrambles in several spots. The trail begins to zig-zag at this point, still heading directly south on average.

Scenery/Points of Interest

Spectacular views to the south and west emerge as the trail climbs toward the summit of the Kittatinny Ridge and the AT. From the base of the Culver Fire Tower there are views in all directions except directly northeast and southwest along the ridge line.

The fire tower is often manned. You may be able to get an invitation to climb up when it is manned.

Climbing

Total elevation gain north to south in 1.45 miles is a little less than 600 feet. The steepest portion is the last 0.15 mile which rises 150 feet for an average slope of 20%. Several short rock scrambles are required at this point.

Maintained by: New York-New Jersey Trail Conference.
Permitted Uses: Between the Stony Brook Trail and Sunrise Mountain Road, hiking, cross-country skiing, hunting, horseback riding, bicycling and snowmobiling are permitted. Between Sunrise Mountain Road and the AT, hiking and cross-country skiing only are permitted.

Stony Brook Trail
1.45 miles, brown blazed

General Description *(map on p. 122)*

Starting near the Stony Lake Day Use Area of Stokes State Forest, the Stony Brook Trail follows Stony Brook upstream, crosses Sunrise Mountain Road at 1.25 miles and ends at the AT on the top of the Kittatinny Ridge at 1.45 miles. A short side trail to the Gren Anderson AT leanto leaves towards

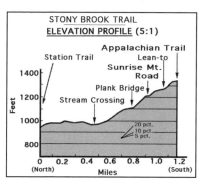

Sunrise Mountain Road

the east at 1.35 miles just 0.15 mile from Sunrise Mountain Road.

Access

The northern terminus is at the Station Trail about 0.45 mile from the large parking area of the Stony Lake Day Use Area. Take the Station Trail from the south end of the parking area following the light green blaze. In 0.15 mile the trail forks (blazed in both directions). Follow the left fork for another 0.3 mile. The Stony Brook Trail begins on the left where the Station Trail begins to loop back to the right. The Stony Brook Trail blazes actually begin at the Stony Lake parking area, so they can be followed from that point.

The trail is also accessible at the Sunrise Mountain Road crossing. Parking is allowed on the right side anywhere along the road, which is one-way. Of course, the trail can also be accessed via the AT.

Trail Surface

The trail begins at the lower, northern end as a wide, smooth woods road. Soon after the intersection with the Station Trail, it changes to a moderately to heavily stoned woods path. The first Stony Brook tributary is crossed just short of 0.8 mile. The last tributary crossing is via a small plank bridge (the only one on the trail) at 1.10 miles. During wet seasons there are also numerous small streams to cross between these two points. The trail is heavily stoned in this area with some minor erosion. After the plank bridge, the trail steepens, climbing up to the Sunrise Mountain Road. Beyond the road, it continues to climb up to the AT at 1.45 miles.

Scenery

Stony Brook is a typical pleasant NJ mountain stream. Views are available from the AT after reaching the south end of the trail.

Climbing

The trail starts almost flat, then rises very gently from 0.3 to 0.8 mile with some ups and downs on an increasingly rough trail. Between 0.8 mile and 1.25 miles it rises 140 feet moderately steeply (7% grade) on a fairly rough trail. This is followed by a short fairly steep climb (18%) up to the Sunrise Mountain Road. Beyond the road another 100-foot climb brings you to the AT. Overall, the trail climbs 400 feet going north to south.

Maintained by: New York-New Jersey Trail Conference
Permitted Uses: From the Station Trail to Sunrise Mountain Road: hiking, horseback riding, hunting, bicycling and cross-country skiing are permitted. From Sunrise Mountain Road to the AT hiking and cross-country skiing only are permitted.

Lackner Trail

2.15 miles, black blazed

General Description *(map on p. 122)*

Starting just 0.2 mile west of the Stony Lake Day Use Area parking lot on Kittle Road, the Lackner Trail generally parallels Coursen Road before turning sharply right, ending just below the Stokes State Forest Headquarters near U.S. 206. The Lead Mine Trail forks off to the right at 0.8 mile from Kittle Road and ends at Coursen Road a third of a mile northwest of the forest headquarters.

Access

Parking is available at the Kittle Road end either at the Stony Lake Day Use Area (0.2 mile) or at the Kittle Field lot (0.25 mile). At the southwest end, parking is available at the headquarters lot, about 0.1 mile from the trail head.

Trail Surface

It is a light to moderately stony woods road for its entire length. Just beyond the Lead Mine Trail junction, the road becomes narrow, approaching a woods path in appearance. At 1.8 miles from the northeast end, the trail crosses a small dam which forms a pond to the left. At that point it turns sharply right, heading for Coursen Road on a very wide and smooth former public road.

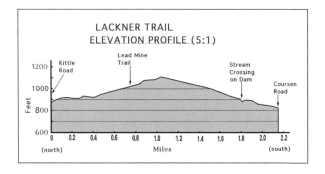

132

Scenery/Points of Interest

There are views of Stony Lake to the left at about 0.2 mile from Kittle Road. An unnamed and unmaintained but blazed trail leaves to the left to circle Stony Lake at 0.2 mile from Kittle Road. This trail terminates at the Coursen Trail on the other side of the lake.

Open hardwood forest predominates, deteriorating almost to scrub forest at the high point of the trail at 1.0 mile from Kittle Road.

Climbing

There is a gentle up slope, climbing a little more than 200 feet from Kittle Road to 1.0 mile, followed by a gradual down slope of 280 feet to the park headquarters.

Maintained by: New York-New Jersey Trail Conference.
Permitted Uses: Hiking, cross-country skiing, hunting, horseback riding, bicycling and snowmobiling.

Lead Mine Trail
0.6 mile, blue over gray blazed

General Description *(map on p. 122)*

The short Lead Mine Trail connects the middle of the Lackner Trail to Coursen Road, effectively providing a short cut to the park headquarters which is a third of a mile beyond the point where the Lead Mine Trail intersects Coursen Road.

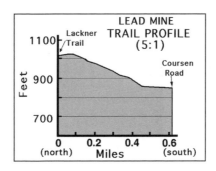

133

Access

One or two cars can be parked at the Coursen Road end. The Lackner Trail end is about a mile from any parking. There is ample parking at the park headquarters, a third of a mile southwest of the Lead Mine trail head on Coursen Road.

Trail Surface

A moderately to lightly stoned woods path.

Scenery

Open hardwood forest with some conifers.

Climbing

There is about a 160-foot descent going from the Lackner Trail to Coursen Road.

Maintained by: New York-New Jersey Trail Conference
Permitted Uses: Hiking, cross-country skiing, hunting, horseback riding, bicycling, snowmobiling.

Tibbs Trail
0.5 mile, blue over green blazed

General Description *(map on p. 122)*

The Tibbs Trail goes almost exactly east/west, connecting Coursen Road to the Shotwell Campground. It passes a swamp which beavers have now converted to a rather large lake on the right side of the trail. There is some

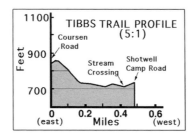

logging activity at the Coursen end of the trail.

Access

There is a parking area in the Shotwell Campground about 0.1 mile from the trailhead and two or three cars can be parked at the Coursen Road trailhead.

Trail Surface

A moderately stony woods road for its entire length. There is a stepping stone crossing of a small stream at 0.4 mile from Coursen Road. Open hardwood forest predominates.

Scenery

Overviews of a large beaver pond in open forest.

Climbing

The trail descends about 150 feet with a moderate slope from Coursen Road to Shotwell Road.

Maintained by: New York-New Jersey Trail Conference.
Permitted Uses: Hiking, cross-country skiing, hunting, horseback riding, bicycling, snowmobiling.

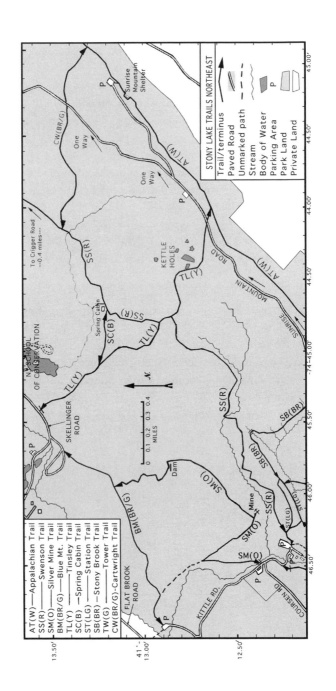

STONY LAKE TRAILS NORTHEAST

Trail/terminus
Paved Road
Unmarked path
Stream
Body of Water
Parking Area
Park Land
Private Land

AT(W) ——Appalachian Trail
SS(R) ———Swenson Trail
SM(O) ——Silver Mine Trail
BM(BR/G)—Blue Mt. Trail
TL(Y) ———Tinsley Trail
SC(B) ——Spring Cabin Trail
ST(LG) ——Station Trail
SB(BR) —Stony Brook Trail
TW(G) ——Tower Trail
CW(BR/G)-Cartwright Trail

CW(BR/G)

Sunrise Mountain Shelter

One Way

One Way

AT(W)

KETTLE HOLES

SS(R)

TL(Y)

MOUNTAIN ROAD

SUNRISE

AT(W)

To Crigger Road
---0.4 miles---

Spring Cabin

SC(B)

SS(R)

TL(Y)

TL(Y)

NJ SCHOOL
OF CONSERVATION

N

SS(R)

SB(BR)

SB(BR)

SKELLINGER
ROAD

0 0.1 0.2 0.3 0.4
MILES

Dam

SM(O)

SS(R)

SS(R)

ST(LG)

ST(LG)

BM(BR/G)

Mine

SM(O)

SM(O)

KITTLE RD.

COURSEN RD.

FLAT BROOK
ROAD

P

P

P

P

P

P

P

45.00'

44.50'

44.00'

74°45.00'

45.50'

46.00'

46.50'

13.50'

41° 13.00'

12.50'

CHAPTER 10

Stony Lake Trails Northeast

- Swenson / *3.9 miles*
- Silver Mine / *2.1 miles*
- Blue Mountain / *1.4 miles*
- Tinsley / *1.95 miles*
- Spring Cabin / *0.3 mile*
- Cartwright / *1.25 miles*
- AT-Culver Tower to Deckertown Pike / *7.0 miles*

T he Swenson Trail starts at the Stony Lake hub on Station Trail and connects to the Steam Mill Camping Area (see following chapter). The Silver Mine and Blue Mountain trails begin on Kittle Road just to the north of the Stony Lake Day Use parking area. All three head generally northeast. The Tinsley and Cartwright trails are remote from the Stony Lake area and are "cross" trails generally heading northwest to southeast and crossing or terminating near the Blue Mountain, Swenson and Applachian trails.

This extensive area is one of gently rolling forested country, lying just below the Kittatinny ridge line and the AT.

Swenson Trail

3.9 miles, red blazed

General Description *(map on p. 136)*

The relatively long and varied Swenson Trail connects the Stony Lake Day Use Area to Crigger Road, not far from Steam Mill Campground (see chapter 11).

The red blazes begin at the west end of the Stony Lake parking area, co-aligned with the Station Trail. In less than 0.1 mile the Swenson Trail veers left on an old woods road as the Station Trail continues straight. The Swenson Trail starts across the top of a small ridge between Stony Brook and a parallel-running tributary in mixed hardwood and hemlock forest. It then drops down off the ridge and crosses the tributary brook at about 1.0 mile. On a winding moderately stony old woods road the trail follows the tributary upstream, finally cresting a low saddle and joining the Tinsley Trail at about 2.0 miles.

Turn left steeply downhill onto the co-aligned Tinsley and Swenson trails. Erosion here has created a very stony surface to the woods road. In a little over 0.1 mile the Swenson Trail veers right onto a fairly steep eroded and heavily stoned foot path. This section gradually flattens out, reaching the "Spring Cabin" and Spring Cabin Trail at a little over 2.4 miles. The cabin is habitable and apparently associated with the State School of Conservation which is just a half-mile to the northwest. A School of Conservation marked path leads in that direction from the cabin.

Continue to follow the red blazes to the east. After passing the Spring Cabin the woods road is wide, smooth and pleasant to follow. The forest is

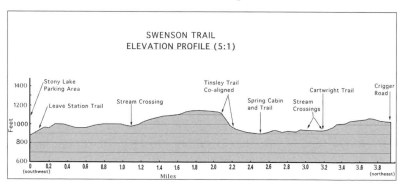

mature hardwood. Approaching an intersection with the Cartwright Trail the Swenson Trail becomes very stony and crosses several minor streams and wet areas, making progress a bit difficult. A signpost for the Cartwright has been placed smack in the middle of the Swenson Trail at 3.1 miles. This is good since one is watching one's feet rather than looking for the Cartwright Trail terminus at this point.

The final section of the Swenson Trail rises gently, first in mature hardwood and then skirting a very young forest which is the result of clear cutting about 30 years ago. This is an excellent illustration of how long it takes for forest to regenerate either from fields or clear cuts. In another 50 years it will be difficult to tell the difference between this forest and a fully mature one.

Access

Primary access is from the Stony Lake parking area and the Station Trail. There is ample parking here as well as a picnic ground, swimming beach and other facilities.

At the north end of the Swenson Trail at Crigger Road several cars can be parked on the roadside. Crigger Road is one way at this point.

The trail can also be accessed via the Tinsley Trail which runs approximately at right angles to the Swenson Trail from Skellinger Road to the AT just west of Sunrise Mountain.

The Cartwright Trail is another access point, but be prepared for a rough trail (see page 148).

Trail Surface

The Station Trail is a wide smooth woods road for 0.1 mile.

Between the Station Trail and the crossing of the Stony Brook tributary at 1.0 mile, there are gradual slopes on a winding woods road with stone cover varying from light to heavy.

Between the tributary crossing and the Tinsley Trail at 2.0 miles, the trail is a moderately stony woods road in mature hardwood forest. Where the Tinsley Trail and Swenson Trail are co-aligned for 0.1 mile, the path is an eroded, heavily stoned steep woods road.

From the Tinsley Trail intersection to the Spring Cabin at 2.4 miles the

Swenson Trail is a heavily stoned path, the slope progressing from steep to flat.

After the Spring Cabin a woods road is picked up again, the slopes are gradual, and the forest is mature hardwood with the trail surface only moderately stony.

In the vicinity of the Cartwright Trail junction at 3.1 miles, the path becomes quite rough, heavily stoned with small stream crossings and wet spots for about 0.2 mile.

The final section from the Cartwright Trail junction to Crigger Road is a pleasant, lightly stoned woods road through 30-year old "new" growth covering a 1970s clear cut logging area.

Scenery/Points of Interest

Stony Lake Day Use Area has a small glacial lake, swimming beach, picnic area and other facilities.

Spring Cabin is beautifully situated in a remote forest location.

Climbing

From the first Tinsley Trail junction to Spring Cabin is a 220-foot descent. Maximum slope is about 18%. All other climbs are very gradual. Overall from southwest to northeast, there is a total of 480 feet of climbing. Going from northeast to southwest, there is a total of 330 feet of climbing.

Maintained by: New York-New Jersey Trail Conference
Permitted Uses: Hiking, horseback riding, hunting, bicycling, snowmobiling.

Silver Mine Trail   *2.1 miles, orange blazed*

General Description *(map on p. 136)*

The interesting and varied Silver Mine Trail connects Kittle Road near where it intersects Coursen Road with the Blue Mountain Trail. It begins by crossing Stony Brook on a foot bridge at a picnic area and then follows the brook downstream for 0.4 mile. At this point the trail takes a sharp right turn onto a woods road which gently climbs away from the brook. This is an easy turn to miss as the woods road following the brook continues onward straight ahead. The only indicator for the turn is the orange trail blazes.

At 0.85 mile the trail splits, with both forks blazed orange. The right fork (actually straight ahead) leads in a short distance to the remains of an old exploratory mine shaft. The left fork (more of a left turn) continues on toward the Blue Mountain Trail.

At 1.6 miles you pass an old concrete dam on the left. The pond it once created is now dry. At this point the trail changes character. It is a relatively newly created extension of the Silver Mine Trail to connect it to the Blue Mountain Trail. It becomes an indistinct winding woods path over somewhat difficult surface and terrain. Following the orange blazes may be tricky at times but is always possible. If you don't immediately see the next blaze after passing the last blaze, stop and search a bit. They were always visible at the time of this writing. This section of trail should become easier to follow with time as trail usage increases and a few more blazes are added.

At 3.1 miles the trail intersects the Blue Mountain Trail. A right turn will take you to Skellinger Road in 0.4 mile. A left turn will take you back in 0.9 mile to Kittle Road where it dead ends nearly a mile from the first trailhead.

Access

There is ample parking across Kittle Road from the trail terminus at the southwest end of the trail. There is also a large parking area off Kittle Road where it dead ends at the western terminus of the Blue Mountain Trail.

Skellinger Road at the eastern end of the Blue Mountain Trail has parking for a few cars at the trail head.

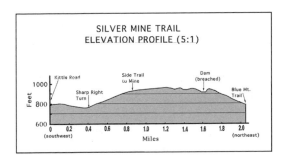

141

Stokes Forest Canopy, looking west from Sunrise Mountain

Trail Surface

The trail is a smooth, wide, almost stone-free woods road for the first 0.85 mile. From there to 1.6 miles it is an older woods road, less wide in places, but still smooth and relatively stone free.

The last half-mile of trail is a newly created woods path with heavy stone cover at some points and moderate or light stone cover at other points. If one of the blazes is destroyed due to a blowdown, the trail may become difficult to follow.

Scenery/Points of Interest

There are the remains of an old exploratory mine shaft (c. 1875) at 0.85 mile. This shaft is most likely a prospector's test dig to determine the extent of the quartz seam which emerges from underground at this location. This seam is rather extensive and can be seen in neighboring rocks in the immediate area. This type of "sugar quartz" is the most common place to find concentrations of precious stones and metal deposits. However, it is unlikely that any precious metals were found.

Stony Brook is quite scenic with small cascades in the first 0.4 mile. There is an old concrete dam and dry pond at 1.6 miles. Open mixed hardwood forest dominates for the entire length.

Climbing

All slopes are gentle, except for a short steep section just beyond the concrete dam.

There is a 180-foot gentle climb from Stony Brook to the trail high point at about 1.25 miles.

The new trail extension to the Blue Mountain Trail descends 160 feet in the last half mile.

Maintained by: New York-New Jersey Trail Conference.
Permitted Uses: Hiking only.

Blue Mountain Trail

1.4 miles, brown over green blazed

General Description *(map on p. 136)*

The Blue Mountain Trail connects Kittle Road with Skellinger Road, generally paralleling Flat Brook Road, a paved public thoroughfare about 0.3 mile to the north. Its west trailhead is at a large parking area near the end of Kittle Road. The trail immediately passes by two ancient preserved barns which are also accessible directly from Kittle Road.

The trail is almost flat, only lightly stoned and easy to follow for its entire length.

The Silver Mine Trail terminates on the right at 0.9 mile from the west end. The east end is reached at 1.4 miles. This trailhead is on a camp road

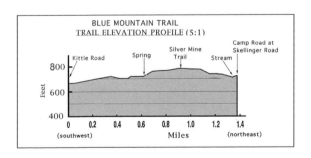

143

(Ocquittunk Campground) just 0.1 mile from Skellinger Road.

Access

A large parking area serves the west trailhead at the end of Kittle Road.

There is parking for a few cars off the camp road at the east terminus. If the campground is crowded, a parking area at a comfort station 0.2 mile northwest on Skellinger Road is the closest alternative. Skellinger Road is also an access point for the Tinsley and the Steam Mill trails. The road is the main access to the State School of Conservation.

Trail Surface

The trail is a lightly stoned undulating woods road for its entire length. The outlet of a small spring at 0.6 mile from the west end and a few small streams in the last half mile are crossed with stepping stones. There are a few blowdowns which need to be circumnavigated as of this writing, but these should be cleared by trail maintainers.

Scenery/Points of Interest

The remains of an old farmstead are quite evident near the western end of the trail. Two ancient preserved barns are just off Kittle Road. The trail traverses old overgrown fields which are quite far along on their reversion to forest. Several huge stone rows are testimony to a great deal of effort to make the old fields viable for crops.

After crossing the stone rows, open hardwood forest dominates with hemlocks appearing as the trail goes east. Hemlocks predominate at the east end.

Climbing

The trail climbs only 110 feet from the west end to the high point at 0.9 mile and then descends only 60 feet to the east terminus.

Maintained by: New York-New Jersey Trail Conference.
Permitted Uses: Hiking, biking, hunting, horseback riding, skiing, snowmobiling.

Tinsley Trail

1.95 miles, yellow blazed

General Description *(map on p. 136)*

The Tinsley Trail climbs moderately and almost continuously 650 feet from Skellinger Road near the State School of Conservation to the AT near the Sunrise Mountain shelter and overlook. The average slope is 7% and it is just short of two miles in length.

For most of its length it follows the path of gravel roads or old woods roads. Overall, negotiating this trail is quite easy.

At 0.5 mile from Skellinger Road, the Spring Cabin Trail (blue blazed) leaves to the left as the Tinsley Trail veers right onto a woods road. The roughest part of the trail is between 1.05 and 1.25 miles where the trail becomes, for a short while, a moderately stony woods path which climbs steeply (up to 20% grade). The Swenson Trail is co-aligned with the Tinsley Trail for much of this section, arriving from the left at 1.05 miles and leaving to the right at 1.15 miles.

The next section of trail is a broad, grassy woods road that leads to a crossing of Sunrise Mountain Road at 1.8 miles. A short (0.1 mile) moderately stony woods path leads from Sunrise Mountain Road to the AT terminus of the Tinsley Trail.

Access

Parking for a few cars can be found at Skellinger Road where the trail terminates. The trail at this point is a gravel road, gated at the Skellinger Road

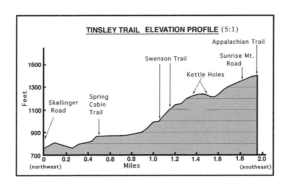

end. Other parking opportunities abound within 1/2 mile of the trailhead on Skellinger Road.

Parking is allowed along the right shoulder of the one-way Sunrise Mountain Road as well.

Trail Surface

From Skellinger Road for the first half mile the path is on a gravel vehicular road. This road veers off to the left at 0.5 mile and leads to Spring Cabin in 0.3 mile. This road is gated (closed) at the Skellinger Road end.

From 0.5 mile to 1.5 miles the trail is a flat to gradually climbing lightly stoned woods road.

From 1.05 to 1.2 miles the old woods road has evolved into a woods path which has a heavily stoned surface due to erosion on the steep slopes of this section.

The last 0.5 mile prior to crossing the Sunrise Mountain Road is a smooth, grassy woods road.

The final 0.1 mile beyond Sunrise Mountain Road to the AT is a moderately stony woods road.

Scenery/Points of Interest

Spring Cabin is 0.3 mile off the trail on a gravel road. It has bunks and a water source. This log cabin appears to have been a small farmstead associated with fairly recently abandoned fields on the Swenson Trail.

Several kettle holes, depressions left by isolated large chunks of melting ice at the end of the last ice age, are scattered not far to the left of the trail in the vicinity of 1.3 to 1.6 miles. Some are water filled in wet seasons. An unmarked trail at 1.4 miles from Skellinger Road leads to several of them. A park brochure describing this area is available at the park headquarters.

Sunrise Mountain is just 0.9 mile northeast of the Tinsley Trail junction with the AT. Views from the shelter at the summit of Sunrise Mountain are spectacular in all directions.

Climbing

From Skellinger Road to the AT is a total net elevation increase of 650

Beemerville Village from Sunrise Mountain

feet. Two slight drops at 0.1 to 0.25 mile and 1.45 to 1.55 miles add another 70 feet to the total climbing.

Maintained by: New York-New Jersey Trail Conference.
Permitted Uses: From Skellinger Road to Swenson Trail: hiking, skiing, horseback riding, bicycling, snowmobiling.
Swenson Trail to Sunrise Mountain Road: hiking, hunting, horseback riding, skiing, bicycling, snowmobiling.
Sunrise Mountain Road to AT: hiking only.

Spring Cabin Trail
0.3 mile, blue blazed

General Description *(map on p. 136)*

This short gravel road leads from the Tinsley Trail at 0.5 mile from Skellinger Road to the Spring Cabin and Swenson trails. It is essentially level. It is maintained by the NY-NJ Trail Conference and has all the usual permitted uses.

Cartwright Trail   *1.25 miles, brown over red blazed*

General Description (*map on p. 136*)

The Cartwright Trail connects the Swenson Trail to the AT, crossing Sunrise Mountain Road in the process. The lower half of the Cartwright Trail in its current condition is recommended for the adventurous only. There are extensive wet areas and erosion on a heavily stoned path combined with a 0.5 mile segment where there are no blazes going west to east. A lot of searching was required in some areas to stay on the trail. The blowdowns and blazing may be rectified, but the erosion, wet spots and stone cover will remain very difficult.

The upper half of the trail is much better. The last 0.25 mile prior to crossing the Sunrise Mountain Road and the 0.4 mile beyond to the AT is well marked, clear and dry.

Access

The western end at the Swenson Trail is more than a mile from the nearest parking area. Fortunately someone has planted a homemade sign in the middle of the Swenson Trail at the Cartwright trailhead; otherwise it could be easily missed since one's concentration at that point (see p. 139) is on one's feet.

The trail crosses Sunrise Mountain Road at 0.85 mile from the western end. From there it is 0.4 mile east to the AT. Parking is allowed on the right shoulder of Sunrise Mountain Road at this crossing.

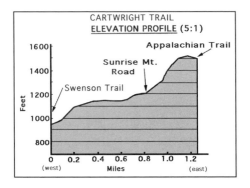

Trail Surface

The westernmost 0.6 mile is extremely rough. The surface is almost 100% large rocks in an area of extensive wetness and erosion.

The last 0.25 mile prior to the Sunrise Mountain Road crossing is a relatively smooth, wide woods road. All of the trail is in mature mixed hardwood forest.

The trail from Sunrise Mountain Road to the AT is a moderately stoned typical woods path. It is rather steep in one spot almost requiring a scramble, but not quite.

Scenery

It provides good access to the AT in the vicinity of Sunrise Mountain with many excellent views.

Climbing

There is 150 feet of climbing in the first 0.2 mile starting at the western end (15% slope average). Another gradual 50 feet brings one to Sunrise Mountain Road.

Between Sunrise Mountain Road and the AT the trail climbs a net 300 feet. One portion is steep enough to almost require a scramble.

Maintained by: New York-New Jersey Trail Conference.
Permitted Uses: Hiking, horseback riding, hunting, bicycling.

APPALACHIAN TRAIL
Sunrise Mt. to Deckertown Pike

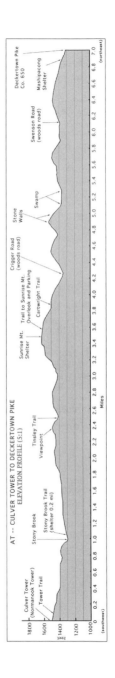

AT -- CULVER TOWER TO DECKERTOWN PIKE
ELEVATION PROFILE (5:1)

View from Sunrise Mountain Shelter

AT- Culver Tower to Deckertown Turnpike

7.0 miles, white blazed

General Description *(see also map p. 136)*

The Culver Tower was formerly known as the Normanook Tower. Although the AT in this section remains generally atop the Kittatinny ridge line, there is nevertheless quite a bit of climbing. The ridge line in this area has lots of ups and downs, as opposed to the long, almost flat runs of the ridge farther south.

The path is a lightly to heavily stoned woods path for basically its entire length. A short stretch (200 feet) is aligned with a woods road at about 6.2 miles from Culver Tower.

In the first four miles the AT is intersected, always from the west, by four Stokes State Forest trails. No marked trails lead east or southeast into the great valley. From a spot about four miles from Culver Tower to Deckertown Turnpike at seven miles the trail is rather remote, being intersected by only two abandoned woods roads.

151

Some of the most spectacular views in the Kittatinnies are available at two major high points, the Culver Tower at 1,510 feet and Sunrise Mountain at 1,650- foot elevation. Sunrise Mountain is the highest point on the AT in the Kittatinny range south of High Point. It's about 1,000 feet above the valley floor to the east and the Delaware River valley to the west.

From the Culver Tower, the path descends gradually for a little more than a mile. The Tower Trail intersects from the left at 0.1 mile from the tower, Stony Brook is crossed at 1.0 mile, and the Stony Brook Trail intersects at about 1.1 miles. The Gren Anderson Shelter is reached by turning left onto the Stony Brook Trail for 0.1 mile and then right onto a blue-blazed trail for another 0.2 mile.

From the Stony Brook Trail there is a very gradual climb to another good viewpoint at 2.4 miles from Culver Tower and 0.1 mile short of the intersection with the yellow blazed Tinsley Trail. From the Tinsley Trail to the pavilion-like shelter at the very top of Sunrise Mountain is another mile on a moderately stony path. Maximum slope as you climb to the top of Sunrise Mountain is about 22%. A tenth of a mile beyond the shelter a short path leads left to a large parking area and overlook (Sunrise Mountain Overlook).

The path then descends 120 feet in a quarter mile to the intersection with the Cartwright Trail, the last of the Stokes State Forest intersecting trails.

Between 4.0 and 7.0 miles from Culver Tower, the trail climbs four small "hills," staying basically atop the ridge line. Each is a 100-foot to 150-foot climb. In the first saddle at 4.3 miles, Crigger Road, now abandoned as a vehicle road, crosses the AT. In the third saddle at 5.2 miles, there is a small swamp to the right (east). Another woods road (Swenson Road) crosses at 6.2 miles in the fourth saddle. There is a final gradual 200-foot descent to Deckertown Turnpike (CO 650).

The large Mashipacong Shelter and an unmarked woods road that connects to the beginning of the Iris Trail is passed 0.1 mile prior to Deckertown Turnpike.

Access

Easiest access to this section of the AT is from the Sunrise Mountain Overlook (off Sunrise Mountain Road) and from Deckertown Turn pike (County

Route 650). Both spots have ample parking on paved roads. The Sunrise Mountain parking area is about 0.1 mile north of the top of Sunrise Mountain at the shelter. The path connecting to the AT leaves from the south end of the parking lot. There are rest rooms here as well. The Deckertown AT parking area is on the north side of the road, across from this section of the AT.

The easiest trail access is from the Tinsley Trail crossing of Sunrise Mountain Road. It is only 0.2 mile and a gentle climb to the AT. Parking is allowed on the right shoulder of the road.

The AT can also be reached by climbing from Sunrise Mountain Road on the Tower, Cartwright or Stony Brook trails (listed in decreasing difficulty). The Tower Trail access is 0.6 mile and a 400-foot climb. The Cartwright Trail to the AT is 0.4 mile and 320 feet and The Stony Brook Trail access is 0.3 mile and 160 feet.

Trail Surface

For almost the entire length, the trail is a light to heavily stoned woods path. Near Sunrise Mountain Overlook the trail is heavily used, smoother and broader than in other areas.

Scenery/Points of Interest

> Culver (Normanook) Fire Tower
> Sunrise Mountain Shelter
> Sunrise Mountain Overlook
> Gren Anderson Shelter
> Mashipacong Shelter

Climbing

Total climbing going SW to NE is 1,050 feet. The biggest climb is up to Sunrise Mountain, a total of 230 feet.

Total climbing going NE to SW is 1,200 feet, with the biggest climb 300 feet up to Sunrise Mountain.

Maintained by: New York-New Jersey Trail Conference.
Permitted Uses: Hiking only.

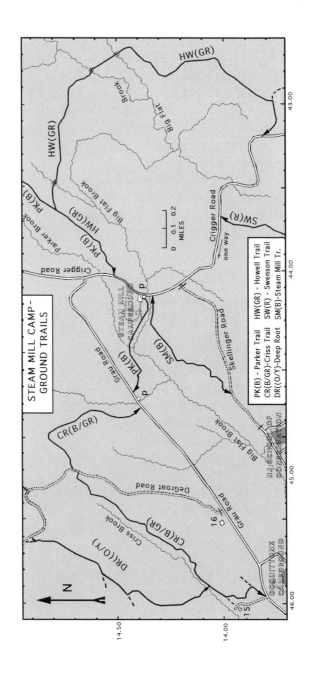

STEAM MILL CAMP-
GROUND TRAILS

PK(B) - Parker Trail   HW(GR) - Howell Trail
CR(B/GR)-Criss Trail   SW(R) - Swenson Trail
DR((O/Y)-Deep Root   SM(B)-Steam Mill Tr.

154

CHAPTER 11

Steam Mill Campground Trails (SSF)

- Steam Mill Trail / *0.8 mile*
- Howell Trail / *2.7 miles*
- Criss Trail / *2.25 miles*
- Deep Root Trail / *1.25 miles*
- Rock Oak Trail / *1.5 miles*
- Parker Trail / *3.7 miles*

These are a group of Stokes State Forest trails which are accessible from Crigger Road and Grau Road. None of these trails intersects the AT. They all lie to the west of the AT and the main Kittatinny ridge line. They are all forest trails under the canopy shown in the photo on page 142. There are few long range views like those found on the Kittatinny ridge trails, but many of the trails traverse beautiful mature forests with pretty streams and small ravines.

The Steam Mill Campground near the intersection of Crigger Road and Grau Road is close to the center of this group of trails. Many of the trails can also be easily accessed from the popular Ocquittunk Campground at the intersection of Grau Road and Skellinger Road.

Most of the Parker Trail actually lies within the borders of High Point State Park but it is closer to this group than to the rest of HPSP trails. The Parker Trail and the AT are the only paths which cross the SSF/HPSP boundary and the Deckertown Turnpike.

Sunrise Mountain Overlook

Steam Mill Trail

0.8 mile, blue blazed

General Description *(map on p. 154)*

The Steam Mill Trail is a short trail which connects Skellinger Road and the State School of Conservation with the Crigger Road Campground and the Parker Trail.

The northeast trailhead where this hike starts is on Crigger Road (which is a two-way road at this point) just across the Big Flat Brook from the Parker Trail and the campground. The trail follows Big Flat Brook for the first quarter mile and then gradually climbs for the next 0.5 mile through fairly recently overgrown fields. The last quarter mile is a slight descent to Skellinger Road.

Access

At this northeast trailhead Skellinger Road is not open to vehicular traffic and is gated at both ends. If you turn right at the south trailhead you will reach the School of Conservation in 0.3 mile. A left turn will take you back to Crigger Road in 0.7 mile at a point 0.2 mile south of your starting point.

There is a large parking area just north of the starting point at Big Flat Brook just across the bridge from the trailhead.

Parking can also be found at the State School of Conservation at the end of the part of Skellinger Road where vehicular traffic is allowed.

Trail Surface

A lightly to moderately stony woods path or partially overgrown woods road the entire length.

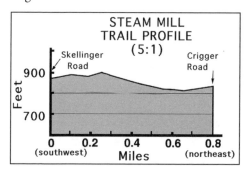

157

Climbing
From where the trail leaves the side of Big Flat Brook to the highest point is a gradual 70-foot climb. The trail then descends about 25 feet to Skellinger Road.

Maintained by: New York-New Jersey Trail Conference
Permitted Uses: Hiking, cross-country skiing, horseback riding, bicycling.

Howell Trail   *2.7 miles, gray blazed*

General Description *(map on p. 154)*
The Howell Trail is a sort of half loop that begins on Crigger Road and returns to Crigger Road just over a mile from the start. At the south end, the trail initially follows an abandoned portion of Crigger Road. The road at one time ran east over the Kittatinny ridge down to the Great Valley, intersecting County Route 519. From the point where the Howell Trail now starts, the road has been abandoned and now cannot be negotiated by most 4WD vehicles. Sunrise Mountain Road ends at the southern Howell Trail terminus and the pavement runs straight ahead onto the surviving paved portion of Crigger Road.

The newly relocated trail follows the badly eroded road uphill for 0.3 mile and then turns left to begin a gradual descent in mature forest on an old woods road. At 1.3 miles a bridge over a tributary of Big Flat Brook is encountered. At 1.4 miles there is a new plank bridge over Big Flat Brook itself.

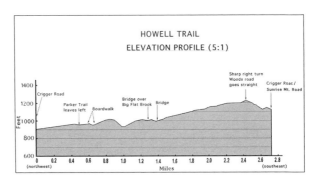

Turkeys in a hay field

At 2.2 miles the Howell Trail joins the Parker Trail which intersects from the right. The two trails are co-aligned until Crigger Road is again reached in another 0.5 mile. The Howell Trail terminates here and the Parker Trail continues, following Crigger Road to the left for 0.2 mile before turning right back into the forest.

Access

Sunrise Mountain Road and the southern portion of Crigger Road are one way west and north. Crigger Road becomes a two-way road at the Steam Mill Campground, just 0.2 mile south of the northern Howell terminus.

Thus the southern Howell Trail terminus cannot be reached from the north. Only by taking Sunrise Mountain Road from US 206 east for about six miles can this end of the trail be reached by car.

At the northern terminus, Crigger Road is two way, so the trail can be reached from the north or south.

Parking is allowed on the right side of Sunrise Mountain Road and Crigger Road where they are one way, so space for several cars is available near the southern terminus of the Howell Trail.

A few cars can also be parked along the road at the northern terminus, but ample parking is available at the Steam Mill Campground parking area 0.2 mile south of the trail terminus.

Trail Surface

The relocated southern 0.3 mile parallels the abandoned Crigger Road. There is a 100 foot climb on this new trail segment.

All of the remainder of the trail is on old woods roads of varying quality. Stone cover ranges from light to moderate, and slopes are generally very gradual except between 0.9 and 1.0 mile from the northern terminus where there is a short slope of about 18%.

Several low wetlands are traversed between the Parker Trail intersection and 1.5 miles from the northern end. There are a few small bridges and boardwalks (puncheons) in this area.

Scenery

The entire trail is in beautiful very mature hardwood forest.

Climbing

The average slope is only 4.6%. Two 80 to 100-foot descents are at 0.9 mile from the north end and at the last 0.3 mile before the southern end of the trail.

Maintained by: New York-New Jersey Trail Conference.
Permitted Uses: Hiking, cross-country skiing, hunting, horseback riding, bicycling.

Criss Trail   *2.25 miles, blue over gray blazed*

General Description *(map on p. 154)*

The Criss Trail starts and ends on Grau Road, crossing the 4-wheel drive DeGroat Road about midway. The southwest end is at the junction of Grau Road and the dirt drive to Stokes State Forest rental cabin no. 15.

From there, it rises gently on a wide woods road for 0.1 mile and then turns abruptly left over a small ridge line, descending to cross a small tributary stream before joining another woods road at about 0.25 mile. The trail turns right, following Criss Brook upstream. An unmarked side trail to the left on a woods road quickly leads to SSF rental cabin no. 15.

At 0.4 mile the newly extended Deep Root Trail joins from the left. The Criss Trail continues upstream, finally reaching 4-wheel drive DeGroat Road where it turns left, following the road for 0.1 mile before turning right back into the woods.

Pine plantations in Stokes State Forest cover abandoned fields.

Here the trail begins a gradual descent, eventually following Forked Brook downstream back to Grau Road at 2.25 miles. This northeastern end of the trail is just 0.1 mile southwest of the Parker Trail terminus on the other side of Grau Road. The two trails can thus be easily combined into an almost continuous forest walk of 6.25 miles.

Access

A few cars can be parked along Grau Road at either end of the trail.

Trail Surface

Like most SSF trails, the Criss Trail follows old woods roads for most of its length. The exception is between 0.1 and 0.25 mile from the southwestern end.

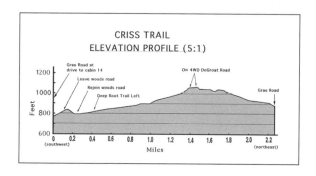

Scenery

The trail is continuously in mature hardwood forest and follows a couple of small mountain streams in shallow ravines.

Climbing

A gradual slope of 1.4 miles between the southwest terminus and DeGroat Road rises a total of 300 feet. From here there is a 200-foot descent back to Grau Road at the northeast terminus.

Maintained by: New York-New Jersey Trail Conference.
Permitted Uses: Hiking, cross-country skiing, hunting, horseback riding, bicycling.

Deep Root Trail   *1.25 miles, orange over yellow blazed*

General Description *(map on p. 154)*

This trail runs from DeGroat Road, which is 4-wheel driveable, to the Criss Trail 0.4 mile from its southern end. The gate at the Grau Road end of DeGroat Road is generally open but the road has been blocked at the west end near the park boundary. The Deep Root Trail northern terminus is about 1.5 miles from Grau Road.

For a hike from Deckertown Turnpike all the way to Grau Road (3.15 miles), the Deep Root can be combined with the Rock Oak Trail which terminates on DeGroat Road 0.4 mile closer to Grau Road, i.e., at 1.1 miles from Grau Road.

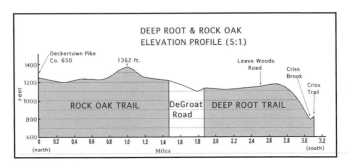

Winterberry flowers and fruit

The Deep Root Trail is perhaps the most level trail in the Kittatinny range for the first 0.9 mile. It follows an old logging road through logged forest that is well on is way back to maturity. Stone cover is light. At 0.9 mile the trail veers left and descends into the ravine with Criss Brook at its bottom. This recently extended section of trail is a moderately to heavily stoned woods path that would be impossible to follow without the excellent blazes. Criss Brook is crossed on a very well constructed small stone path at 1.2 miles, and the trail terminates on the Criss Trail just beyond at 1.25 miles. Turn right on the Criss Trail and you can get to cabin no. 15 in 0.2 mile or the end of the Criss Trail on Grau Road in 0.4 mile.

Access

There is parking for only one or two cars at the north end of the trail or the south end of the Criss Trail. Several cars can be parked at cabin no. 15

provided the current occupants (if any) don't mind.

Trail Surface

The 0.9 mile of logging road is broad and grassy with essentially no rocks. The 0.35 mile descending the side of the ravine is a moderately to heavily stoned woods path that can be followed only by referring to the blazes which are fortunately excellent here.

Scenery

The trail goes through forest which appears to have been selectively cut about 30 to 50 years ago. The Criss Brook ravine is in more mature hardwood forest.

Climbing

For 0.9 mile the trail is almost exactly level. In the last 0.35 mile it descends almost 400 feet to Criss Brook.

Maintained by: New York-New Jersey Trail Conference
Permitted Uses: Hiking, cross-country skiing, hunting, horseback riding, bicycling, snowmobiling.

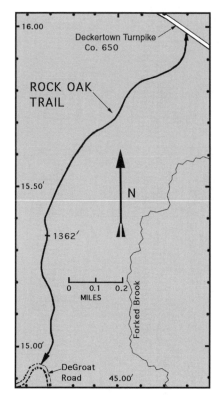

Rock Oak Trail

1.5 miles, blue over yellow blazed

General Description

A trail of gentle slopes in a forest which was variously clear cut, or selectively cut from 10 to 40 years ago, depending on the exact area. It is a companion trail to the Deep Root Trail, terminating just 0.4 mile east of the Deep Root Root trailhead at DeGroat Road.

The Rock Oak Trail runs from Deckertown Turnpike (County Route 650) to DeGroat Road. The Rock Oak Trail and the Deep Root Trail are among the most isolated in Stokes State Forest.

Access

One or two cars can be parked at the DeGroat Road end, several cars at the Deckertown Turnpike end.

Trail Surface

The entire length is a lightly stoned, wide, smooth logging road.

Scenery

Various clear cut or selectively cut hardwood forest areas which seem to have been logged between 10 and 40 years ago, depending on the exact location. Actually the forest is now quite mature and pleasant to walk through.

Climbing

The trail goes directly over a small ridge line, climbing about 150 feet in

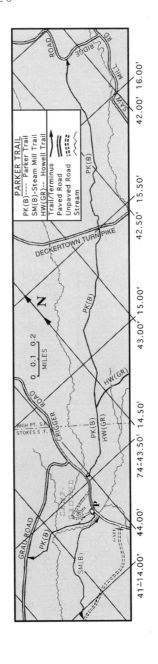

0.7 mile to a maximum of 1,362 feet at the top. The trail then descends about 120 feet to DeGroat Road in 0.6 mile.

Maintained by: New York-New Jersey Trail Conference.
Permitted Uses: Hiking, cross-country skiing, hunting, horseback riding, bicycling, snowmobiling.

Parker Trail
3.7 miles, green blazed

General Description

The Parker Trail and the AT are the only two trails which connect Stokes State Forest and High Point State Park, and the only trails which cross Deckertown Turnpike (County Route 650).

The Parker is a relatively long trail for the Kittatinny, having three distinct sections:

(1) From Park Ridge Road in HPSP to the Deckertown Turnpike the trail is on a wide old woods road. It rises gently about 50 feet and then descends gradually about 130 feet to Deckertown Turnpike. This section is 1.2 miles long. Parker Brook is a quarter mile to the right and Big Flat Brook is a quarter mile to the left.

(2) From Deckertown Turnpike to Crigger Road the trail continues a very gradual descent (200 feet in 1.7 miles) on a woods road. The Howell Trail (see below) joins from the left at 1.2 miles from Deckertown Turnpike and is co-aligned with the Parker up to Crigger Road. The length of this section is 1.7 miles.

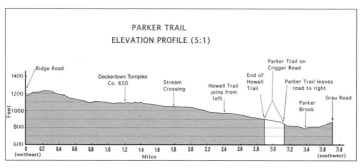

(3) The trail turns left onto Crigger Road and follows it for 0.2 mile where it turns right into the woods just beyond the Steam Mill Campground parking area. For the next 0.1 mile the trail winds up and down along Big Flat Brook in scrub forest. This portion of the trail is very difficult to follow and to negotiate. There is heavy stone cover and many up and down slopes. It can be avoided by taking the campground road at the far end of the Steam Mill parking area for about 100 yards and then following an unmarked trail to the left for another 100 yards where it intersects the Parker Trail along the bank of Big Flat Brook.

The next 0.1 mile of the Parker Trail is in a beautiful mature hemlock forest along Big Flat Brook. At 0.2 mile the trail crosses Parker Brook where it flows into Big Flat Brook. The crossing is on stepping stones and can be quite difficult in high water.

Finally the trail ascends 70 feet in 0.3 mile to Grau Road.

Access

The trail can be accessed from Park Ridge Road in HPSP, Deckertown Turnpike, Crigger Road and Grau Road.

The most difficult parking is at Grau Road. Only one or two cars can be parked along the road at the trail terminus.

At Crigger Road there is ample parking at the Steam Mill Campground parking area as well as along the road.

The Deckertown Turnpike road crossing point has space for a few cars on both sides of the road.

Park Ridge Road has space for one or two cars along the road at the trail terminus, but more room in small pull-outs within 0.1 mile of the terminus.

Trail Surface

The trail surface is a lightly to moderately stony woods path for most of its length. However, the first 0.1 mile after Crigger Road is heavily stoned, tortuous, and rough.

Scenery

Big Flat Brook and Parker Brook are relatively pristine mountain streams. Much of the trail is in open, mature hardwood forest.

Climbing

There is a 430-foot difference between the high point and the low point on the trail. But all slopes are very gradual, never exceeding 10% for long.

Maintained by: New York-New Jersey Trail Conference.
Permitted Uses: Hiking, cross-country skiing, hunting, horseback riding, bicycling, snowmobiling, dog sledding.

View of the Kittatinnies from the Great Valley

CHAPTER 12

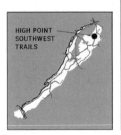

High Point Trails Southwest (HPSP)

- Iris Trail / *4.3 miles*
- AT-NJ 23 to Deckertown Turnpike / *4.6 miles*
- Mashipacong Trail / *2.7 miles*
- Blue Dot Trail / *0.4 mile*
- Ayers Trail / *1.0 mile*
- Fuller Trail / *0.85 mile*
- Life Trail / *0.75 mile*

Topographically the southwestern portion of High Point State Park is an extension of Stokes State Forest. Where they meet the park lands cover not only the Kittatinny ridge line, but also the parallel ridges to the west and northwest, an area up to six miles wide compared to the typical three miles. Toward the northeast all of the ridges increase somewhat in elevation, culminating at the High Point Monument at over 1,800 feet.

Two major access roads cross the ridges east to west, the Deckertown Turnpike (County Route 650) and NJ State Route 23. But only two trails cross the Deckertown Turnpike, the Parker Trail and the AT. Most other trails in this section are accessible from two connector roads, Saw Mill Road and Park Ridge Road. The Iris Trail generally parallels the AT and runs between the Deckertown Turnpike and Route 23.

The Iris and AT combined can be an excellent loop hike. It is a total of nine miles, but there are several ways to shorten the hike as the Iris and the AT cross four times.

Another interesting loop hike of 6.7 miles is to combine the Mashipacong Trail with the AT, the Blue Dot Trail, and the Ayers Trail. See the map on page 178.

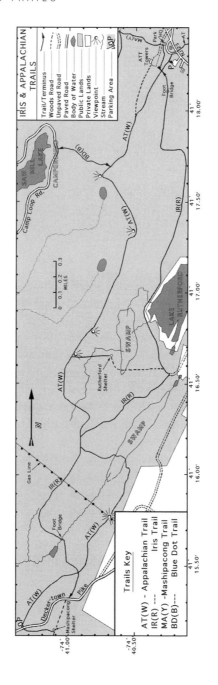

172

Iris Trail

4.3 miles, red blazed

General Description

High Point State Park's longest trail other than the AT, the Iris Trail stretches from State Route 23 near the park headquarters to the Deckertown Turnpike (County Route 650). Since the best access to the trailhead is from the parking area near the park headquarters, this trail is described from north to south.

It is a relatively easy trail with mostly gentle slopes and broad woods roads without major stone cover.

Starting at the AT parking lot just east of the High Point State Park headquarters on Route 23, the trail intersects the AT in about 100 feet. It remains co-aligned with the AT for less than 0.1 mile. At this point there is a trail "crossroads", with the Mashipacong Trail to the right, the Iris Trail to the left and the AT straight ahead. All are well marked.

At 0.25 mile there is a small footbridge across a swampy area. The trail undulates up and down through mature hardwood forest which gradually turns to scrub forest as the trail becomes more stony.

At 1.5 miles Lake Rutherford becomes visible to the left. The trail follows the lake shore about 150 feet away until 2.0 miles. Two lake inlet streams are crossed in this section as well.

The Rutherford AT shelter access road enters from the right at 2.3 miles and the Iris Trail turns right away from the road about 100 yards beyond.

The AT joins from the right and is coaligned with the Iris Trail from 3.0 miles to 3.1 miles.

There is another footbridge across a small stream at 3.8 miles and the AT

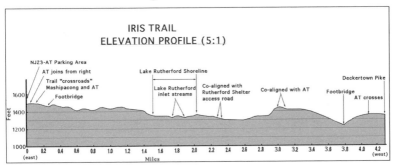

crosses the Iris Trail one last time at 4.1 miles.

The trail ends at a small parking area on Deckertown Road.

Access

There is ample parking in the AT parking area off NJ State Route 23 just east of the High Point State Park headquarters.

The AT crosses or is coaligned with the Iris Trail for short stretches in three locations. So combining the AT and the Iris in a loop hike of various lengths is possible.

There is parking for several cars at the Deckertown Turnpike end.

Trail Surface

The entire trail is on woods roads with stone cover varying from none to moderately heavy.

A short piece of the trail is on the Rutherford Shelter access road.

Two footbridges cross streams, but there are several streams and wet spots which require stepping from stone to stone.

Scenery/Points of Interest

Most of the trail is in mature hardwood forest, with some of the more exposed or stony sections in scrub forest with trees reaching a height of only 30 to 40 feet rather than the typical 70-to-90-foot canopy height.

Climbing

The trail undulates up and down with generally gradual slopes for the first 2.0 miles starting from NJ State Route 23.

From 2.9 to 3.0 miles there is a 150-foot climb. The trail then descends 200 feet to a small brook at 3.8 miles and immediately climbs back another 150 feet before ending at Deckertown Turnpike.

Maintained by: New York-New Jersey Trail Conference.
Permitted Uses: Hiking, skiing, horseback riding, bicycling, dog sledding and snowmobiling.

AT-NJ Route 23 to Deckertown Turnpike *4.6 miles, white blazed*

General Description *(map on p. 172)*

Descending into a high saddle in the Kittatinny ridge occupied by NJ State Route 23, the AT emerges from the woods on the north side of the highway, crosses a small field or lawn, crosses the highway and then crosses the lawn of the High Point State Park headquarters building, after which it reenters the forest. In a few hundred feet a side trail to the left leads to a special AT parking area which is entered from Route 23 southeast of the park headquarters. This parking area is where most day hikes on this portion of the AT will start, since only short term parking is available at the park headquarters. Like the Iris trail above, this trail is described from north to south.

Between this point and a trail "crossroads" about 0.1 mile distant, the AT is joined by the Mashipacong and Iris Trails, both of which terminate at the parking area. At the trail "crossroads," the AT continues on straight, while the Mashipacong Trail goes right and the Iris Trail goes left.

At about 0.4 mile, the AT climbs 150 feet to the top of the ridge. At 0.9 mile the Blue Dot Trail goes right steeply downhill, ending at the Saw Mill Pond campground 350 feet below.

A good viewpoint to the west overlooking Saw Mill Pond is 0.1 mile after this trail junction.

The trail then descends 150 feet into a low area between two ridges and immediately climbs back up about 180 feet to the top of the next ridge. There is another good viewpoint at the ridge top at 1.4 miles.

At 2.3 miles the trail skirts a large boulder called Dutch Shoe Rock. There

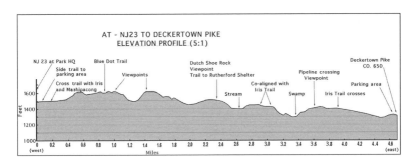

High Point State Park Headquarters

are views in all directions and a blue blazed side trail leads 0.4 mile downhill to the Rutherford Shelter.

The Iris Trail again crosses the AT between 2.9 and 3.0 miles. The two trails are co-aligned for about 350 feet.

Another descent of about 150 feet follows to a low swampy area which is crossed on stepping stones and puncheons.

A final ascent to a pipeline crossing (3.8 miles) and a view over the Great Valley is followed by a gradual descent, crossing the Iris Trail one more time (at 4.2 miles) and finally reaching a parking area on Deckertown Turnpike (CO 650) at 4.8 miles.

Access

There are excellent parking areas at both ends of this section of the AT. The trail can also be accessed from the Mashipacong and Blue Dot trails to the northwest. The Iris Trail is a generally parallel trail which crosses the AT in three places.

Trail Surface

The trail is a well used woods path for almost its entire length. Stone cover is mostly moderate to heavy, with heavy stone cover most common on the northern half of the trail.

A short section where the AT is co-aligned with the Iris Trail is an old woods road.

Scenery/Points of Interest

The High Point State Park headquarters is worth a visit. There are several good viewpoints on this section of the AT in both westerly and easterly directions.

Climbing

There are five or six short 100-to-200-foot climbs or descents but no large climbs. The climb up to the second ridge is close to being a rock scramble.

Maintained by: New York-New Jersey Trail Conference.
Permitted Uses: Hiking only.

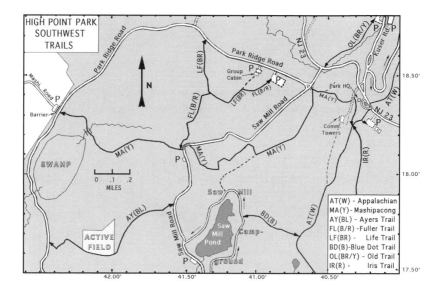

HIGH POINT PARK
SOUTHWEST
TRAILS

AT(W) - Appalachian
MA(Y)- Mashipacong
AY(BL) - Ayers Trail
FL(B/R) -Fuller Trail
LF(BR) -   Life Trail
BD(B)-Blue Dot Trail
OL(BR/Y) - Old Trail
IR(R) -   Iris Trail

Mashipacong Trail

2.7 miles, yellow/blue blazed

General Description

A highly varied and quite high altitude (above 1200 feet) trail, the Mashipacong Trail consists of five distinct sections.

Between the trailhead at Park Ridge Road and the crossing at Saw Mill Road is a pleasant 0.9 mile walk on an old woods road with gentle slopes.

Between Saw Mill Road and an old paved road now a fire road, the trail remains basically flat following a winding path through overgrown fields in various stages of reforestation. This section is 0.6 mile long.

The trail follows the unnamed fire road for another 0.6 mile to a gate at the intersection of Saw Mill and Park Ridge roads. This portion is smooth, broad and gently upward sloping.

The trail again enters the woods at the gate, this time as a distinct woods path. It climbs a 150-foot bluff and intersects the access road between NJ State Route 23 and the AT&T towers at 0.4 mile from the gate.

The last section crosses the tower access road, drops down a bank, skirts the backyard of the High Point State Park headquarters and ends at a junction with the AT. Straight ahead is the beginning of the Iris Trail.

Actually both the Mashipacong and Iris trails are blazed continuously with the AT to the left. In 300 feet, a short side trail leads to a large parking area another 150 feet beyond, where both the Mashipacong and Iris blazes terminate.

Access

At the western end on Park Ridge Road, there is parking for a few cars only. There is a large parking area just over a barrier, but this is not directly accessible from Park Ridge Road. It is the end of a paved public road portion of Mashipacong Road.

There is parking for a few cars in a lot on the west side of Saw Mill Road about 200 feet south of where the Mashipacong Trail crosses the road.

No parking is allowed at the intersection of Park Ridge and Saw Mill Roads. The nearest parking area is 0.3 mile down Park Ridge Road on the left side.

The park headquarters has only short-term parking. All AT and trail parking is directed to a large "AT Lot" 0.1 mile west of the headquarters off NJ State Route 23.

Trail Surface

Between Park Ridge Road and Saw Mill Road is a broad old woods road lightly to moderately stoned.

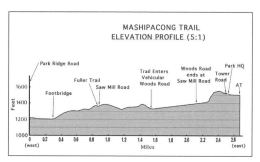

Between Saw Mill Road and the gated fire road is a lightly stoned woods and field path.

The gated fire road is broad, smooth and partially paved. From the gate to the terminus at the AT is a moderately stony woods path, which is actually a woods road that has been growing back for many years. The steep climb up the 150-foot bluff in this section is moderately eroded.

Scenery/Points of Interest

A relatively mature open hardwood forest predominates for most of the length of the trail. Between Saw Mill Road and the gated fire road, the forest is much younger, in some places skirting recently overgrown fields.

A red fox looking for lunch

The High Point State Park headquarters is worth a brief visit.

Climbing

The eastern terminus is 300 feet higher than the western terminus. All slopes are quite gentle except for the 150-foot climb up the bluff 0.3 to 0.2 mile from the eastern terminus.

Maintained by: New York-New Jersey Trail Conference.
Permitted Uses: Hiking, cross-country skiing, horseback riding, bicycling, snowmobiling and dog sledding.

Blue Dot Trail

0.4 mile, blue blazed

General Description *(map on p. 178)*

A short trail connecting the Saw Mill Campground with the AT, the Blue Dot is the most difficult trail in High Point State Park.

It rises 340 feet in 0.4 mile for an average slope of 16.2%. It starts at the campground end in a short swampy area bridged by puncheons (boardwalks). It then begins to rise gradually. The slope increases continuously, going to over 40% as the trail nears the AT. This is a rock scramble or near rock scramble slope.

Don't confuse this trail with the Worthington Blue Dot Trail which ascends Mt. Tammany at the Delaware Water Gap.

Access

There is parking available at the campground end and the trail can be accessed from the AT just 0.9 mile from the AT parking area off NJ State Route 23.

Trail Surface

Except for a short piece on boardwalks at the campground (western) end, the trail is heavily to completely stoned, generally getting stonier as it approaches the AT. The last 0.1 mile is basically a rock scramble.

Scenery

Good views from the top and interesting rock formations if you are interested in a small challenge.

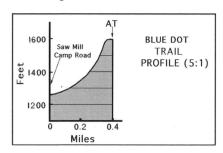

181

Climbing
A gradually steepening climb of 340 feet in 0.4 mile, starting at 0% slope and ending at over 40% slope.

Maintained by: New York-New Jersey Trail Conference.
Permitted Uses: Hiking only.

Ayers Trail
1.0 mile, black blazed

General Description *(map on p. 178)*
The Ayers Trail is a pleasant one-mile walk in woods and field. It runs east to west from Park Ridge Road to Saw Mill Road. Woods roads are followed for the entire length; the eastern portion of the trail is still used for access to an agriculturally active field about 1/2 mile from Saw Mill Road.

The trail rises gently from Park Ridge Road in mature hardwood forest to the field mentioned above at 0.25 mile. It follows the edge of the field for another 0.25 mile before re-entering the hardwood forest. From that point to Saw Mill Road, 0.5 mile, the trail is almost level.

Access
There is no specific parking area at either end of the trail, but one or two cars can be parked along the road at each end. There is a larger parking area about 0.25 mile north on Saw Mill Road or about 0.5 mile south at Saw Mill Pond.

Trail Surface
Broad, smooth woods road for the entire length.

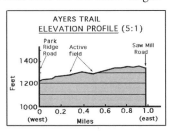

182

Scenery

Mature hardwood forest and an agriculturally active field.

Climbing

A total gradual climb of 250 feet is required from Park Ridge Road to Saw Mill Road.

Maintained by: New York-New Jersey Trail Conference
Permitted Uses: Hiking, cross-country skiing, horseback riding, bicycling, snowmobiling and dog sledding.

Fuller Trail   *0.85 mile, red over blue blazed*

General Description *(map on p. 178)*

The Life and Fuller trails start co-aligned at the southwest corner of the winter sports parking area off Park Ridge Road. At 0.2 mile an unmarked woods road to the right leads to the Group Camp Cabin. At 0.4 mile the Life Trail goes straight ahead and the Fuller Trail makes a sharp left turn. At 0.85 mile the Fuller Trail intersects the Mashipacong Trail about 30 feet from Saw Mill Road.

Access

Ample parking exists at the winter sports parking area off Park Ridge Road and there is parking for several cars on Saw Mill Road 0.1 mile south of where the Fuller and Mashipacong trails meet it.

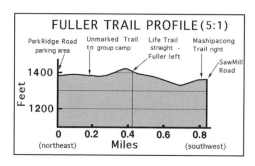

Trail Surface

The first 0.2 mile from the northern end is a lightly stoned woods path. The next 0.2 mile is on a broad lightly stoned woods road. After the sharp left turn, the trail is on a narrow, very old moderately stony woods road.

Scenery

The trail is in mature hardwood forest severely damaged in the 2003 ice storm.

Climbing

The south end is about 20 feet lower than the north end. There is very little overall climbing.

Maintained by: New York-New Jersey Trail Conference.
Permitted Uses: Hiking, cross-country skiing, horseback riding, bicycling, snowmobiling and dog sledding.

Life Trail

0.8 mile, brown blazed

General Description *(map on p. 178)*

A short easy trail associated with the Stokes State Forest Group Camping Area, the Life Trail runs from Park Ridge Road back to the same road 0.5 mile further on.

The trailhead is at the winter sports parking area off Park Ridge Road,

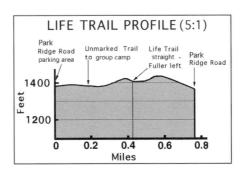

just to the east of the Stokes State Forest Group Camping Area. At this point the Life Trail and the Fuller Trail (see page 184) are co-aligned. Both start at the southwest corner of the large parking area as a lightly stoned woods path.

In 0.2 mile an unmarked woods road enters from the right. The group camp cabin is 0.15 mile to the right and both trails follow the woods road to the left. At 0.4 mile the Fuller and Life trails part company, the Fuller Trail taking a sharp left turn on a very old woods road and the Life Trail continuing straight ahead. At 0.8 mile the Life Trail again intersects Park Ridge Road. If you turn right on Park Ridge Road, you will get back to the starting point parking area in 0.5 mile. Traffic on Park Ridge Road is very light.

Access
Ample parking exists at the winter sports parking area at the east terminus. One or two cars can be parked along the road at the west terminus.

Trail Surface
Broad, smooth, lightly stoned woods road for 0.55 mile and a lightly stoned woods path for about 0.25 mile.

Scenery
Mature hardwood forest.

Climbing
This trail is almost level. The west end is about 20 feet lower than the east end. A 40-foot gradual rise must be negotiated between.

Maintained by: New York-New Jersey Trail Conference.
Permitted Uses: Hiking, cross-country skiing, horseback riding, bicycling, snowmobiling and dog sledding.

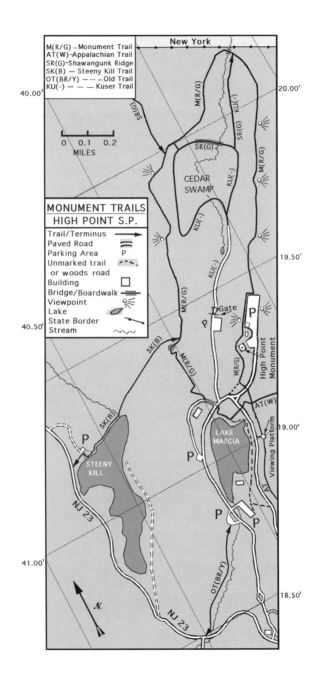

MONUMENT TRAILS
HIGH POINT S.P.

M(R/G) —Monument Trail
AT(W)–Appalachian Trail
SR(G)-Shawangunk Ridge
SK(B) — Steeny Kill Trail
OT(BR/Y) — — —Old Trail
KU(-) — — — Kuser Trail

Trail/Terminus
Paved Road
Parking Area   P
Unmarked trail
 or woods road
Building
Bridge/Boardwalk
Viewpoint
Lake
State Border
Stream

CHAPTER 13

High Point Monument Trails (HPSP)

•AT-NJ 23 to High Point Monument / *1.1 miles*
•Monument Trail / *3.55 miles*
•Steeny Kill Trail / *0.7 mile*
•Old Trail / *0.5 mile*
•Kuser Trail / *1.9 miles*
•AT & Shawangunk Ridge Trails beyond High Point Monument

T he High Point Monument is a 220-foot granite obelisk sitting atop the highest point in New Jersey. It is hollow cored just like the Washington Monument in D.C., but climbing to the top has not been allowed for several years awaiting a renovation of the internal staircase. Built in 1928 to 1930, it is visible from great distances (up to 30 miles) and from many of the trails described in this guide.

The Monument Trail loop described here passes by the obelisk. Connected to the Monument Trail are the AT, the Steeny Kill Trail, the unmarked Kuser Trail and the well marked Shawangunk Ridge Trail which heads into New York state where our Kittatinny Mountain changes names. New Yorkers think of the Kittatinny ridge as an extension of the Shawangunks. New Jerseyans think of the Shawangunks as an extension of the Kittatinnies.

AT–State Route 23 to High Point Monument

1.1 miles, white blazed

General Description (maps on pp. 178, 186)

After crossing NJ State Route 23 at the High Point State Park Headquarters, the AT traverses an open field and then climbs back to the top of the Kittatinny ridge. It generally parallels the one-way park road known as "Scenic Drive," following the ridge top until it reaches a local high point (1,680 feet) where a large observation platform has been built (at 0.95 mile from NJ State Route 23) overlooking Lake Marcia. The platform is raised about 25 feet above ground, enough height to clear the scrubby forest on the ridge top. The trail then descends to about 1,600 feet where it "kisses" the Monument Trail (see below) and makes a sharp right turn, descending the Kittatinny ridge to cross the Great Valley of the Appalachians to the Appalachian Highlands of New Jersey.

Access

There is a large AT parking area just southwest of the park headquarters off NJ State Route 23. A very short side trail leads immediately to the AT. Turn right and you will immediately cross Route 23 onto this section of the trail. It can also be accessed from the park headquarters lot but there is a time limit on parking there.

Scenic Drive provides access directly to the viewing platform at 0.95 mile. There is parking for a few cars along the road and a short side trail heads 100 feet up the hill to the AT and the viewing platform.

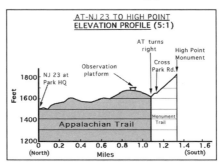

NJ 23 looking east to HPSP

The AT also meets the Monument Trail just 1/4 mile from the High Point Monument. The two trails make a crossroads in the woods, the AT forming the south and east legs of the cross and the Monument Trail forming the west and north legs (see map p. 186). The Monument Trail climbs 220 feet in the 0.25 mile from this point to the monument (17% grade).

Trail Surface

A moderately stony woods path for most of its length in mature or scrubby hardwood forest, depending on elevation.

Scenery/Points of Interest

The view from the observation platform is almost as spectacular as the view from the High Point Monument. Lake Marcia below to the west is an added attraction.

The High Point Monument is easily accessible from this trail. A hike from the parking area on NJ State Route 23 to the monument is a scenic combination hike.

Climbing

From NJ State Route 23 to the ridge top is a 100-foot climb. Then another 80 feet is needed to get to the observation platform.

From the Monument Trail to the observation platform is an 80-foot climb.

Maintained by: New York-New Jersey Trail Conference.
Permitted Uses: Hiking only.

Monument Trail

3.55 miles, red over green blazed

General Description *(map on p. 186)*

A loop trail that touches the High Point obelisk, the New York border and little Lake Marcia, the Monument Trail is among the most popular trails in the Kittatinny range.

A good place to start is in the High Point Monument parking area. There are views in all directions from the lot. Proceeding northeast along the ridge line, there are multiple views of the Great Valley, especially in winter.

The trail then descends to the north, crossing a small stream over a bridge at 1.1 miles and looping back to the southwest just short of the New York – New Jersey border.

At 1.7 miles from the monument parking area, the Shawangunk Ridge Trail leaves to the right. This trail will eventually extend along the Shawangunk Ridge to the Long Path, 36 miles to the north.

Views to the northwest toward Pennsylvania now emerge, until the path again descends to a small stream and to the Steeny Kill Trail on the right at 2.45 miles.

Beyond the stream, crossed on a footbridge, the trail rises steeply on rock steps. The climb is almost 300 feet and the slope about 20%, but the stone steps make it relatively easy going.

Next the trail descends about 100 feet to a park road which it follows for 100 yards before crossing Kuser Road to the shore of Lake Marcia. It follows the northeast shore of the lake for about 200 yards and veers left up the hillside on a very rough trail. It crosses Scenic Drive park road and contacts the AT at

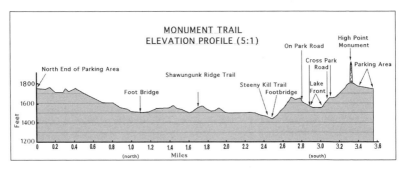

3.1 miles, then veers left to cross another park road before finally ascending to the High Point Monument.

It is about a 250-foot climb from Lake Marcia to the monument done in about 0.3 mile (17% average slope). The Shawangunk Trail, in theory, starts where the AT contacts the Monument Trail and is co-aligned with the Monument and Kuser trails before leaving to the north. However, there is little or no blazing to indicate this.

High Point Monument

Access

Easiest access is from the High Point Monument parking area, but the trail can also be accessed from lower parking areas around Lake Marcia. And, of course, the AT, the Shawangunk Ridge Trail and the Steeny Kill all intersect it.

The park-maintained but unmarked Kuser Trail (see below) through the cedar swamp lies wholly within the loop of the Monument Trail and intersects it in two spots, one at the stream crossing near the New York border, and another just before the Shawangunk Ridge Trail.

Trail Surface

From the monument parking area, all the way to the second stream crossing near the Steeny Kill Trail intersection, the trail is a moderate to lightly stony woods path.

The climb after the second stream crossing is mostly on rock steps, obviously installed with a great deal of work many years ago (probably by the CCC).

191

Port Jervis, New York

Along Lake Marcia the trail is wider and practically stone free. When the trail veers away from the lake before ascending the final High Point Monument hill, it is extremely rough with many large boulders and is totally stone covered in sections. This part of the trail can be easily avoided, however, simply by walking the park roads back to the monument.

Scenery/Points of Interest

High Point State Park lands were donated by Colonel Anthony and Susie Dryden Kuser in 1923. The highest point in New Jersey is marked by the obelisk-shaped 220-foot-tall monument, the base of which is at 1,803 feet above sea level. Views from the monument and from the area surrounding it are quite spectacular, including the towns of Port Jervis, New York and Matamoras, Pennsylvania. The tower construction was completed in 1930.

Lake Marcia is a spring-fed natural lake and has a swimming beach.

The Cedar Swamp area inside the loop of the Monument Trail is preserved as a "natural area." It is timbered with eastern white cedar. A self-guided trail booklet is available from the park headquarters.

Climbing

There are two steep climbs already mentioned, one just southwest of the Steeny Kill Trail, and a second just prior to the monument itself. Each is about

250 feet with slopes in the 15% to 20% range. All other slopes are quite gradual. From the lowest point on the trail to the highest point at the monument is 350 feet.

Maintained by: New York-New Jersey Trail Conference
Permitted Uses: Hiking, cross-country skiing.

Steeny Kill Trail   *0.7 mile, blue blazed*

General Description *(map on p. 186)*

This trail connects the Monument Trail to Steeny Kill Lake and NJ State Route 23. It starts at that highway and immediately drops down to the lake shore at a boat launch, 0.1 mile from the trailhead. It then follows the top of the Steeny Kill Lake dam that has been recently refurbished. After crossing the lake outlet stream on stones, the trail enters the woods, rising gradually at first and then more steeply just before intersecting the Monument Trail.

Access

The trail can be accessed from the Monument Trail about 0.3 mile from Kuser Road.

The boat launch area near the NJ State Route 23 end of the trail is accessed by a gravel road that ends in an ample parking area.

Trail Surface

The short section of trail between NJ State Route 23 and the boat launch

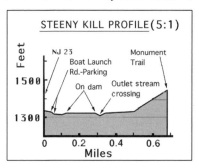

193

parking area is a smooth, gradually descending foot path.

Between the boat launch and the crossing of the lake outlet at 0.3 mile, the trail is on top of the recently refurbished dam. It is wide, smooth and grassy, and recently blazed.

Beyond the lake the trail enters a very mature hardwood forest on a moderately to lightly stoned path. It ascends toward the Monument Trail in the last 0.2 mile of the trail.

Scenery

Steeny Kill Lake is the largest lake wholly within High Point State Park.

Climbing

The trail ascends 140 feet in the last 0.2 mile before intersecting the Monument Trail.

Maintained by: New York-New Jersey Trail Conference
Permitted Uses: Hiking, horseback riding, bicycling, cross-country skiing.

Old Trail
0.5 mile, brown over yellow blazed

General Description *(map on p. 186)*

A short trail that connects the Lake Marcia beach parking area with NJ State Route 23 at Saw Mill Road, the Old Trail is extensively used for cross-country skiing in winter. The High Point ski concession keeps the trail in excellent condition.

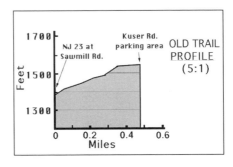

Access

The Lake Marcia beach parking area is across Kuser Road from the trail head. There is also a large gravel parking lot associated with a picnic area right at the trail head. Parking at the NJ State Route 23 end is limited, but a couple of spots can be found off Saw Mill Road just beyond the trail head. No other trails intersect the Old Trail.

Trail Surface

A smooth, grassy, wide woods road.

Scenery

Open mixed hardwood forest.

Climbing

The trail descends 160 feet from Kuser Road to NJ State Route 23.

Maintained by: New York-New Jersey Trail Conference
Permitted Uses: Hiking, cross-country skiing, horseback riding, bicycling.

Kuser Trail
1.9 miles, not blazed

General Description *(map on p. 186)*

The Dryden Kuser Natural Area preserves a very unusual high elevation cedar bog. The trail circumnavigates the bog forming a roughly circular loop in the middle of the trail sequence from Kuser Road to the Monument Trail near the New Jersey-New York border.

The bog is quite fantastic, especially in a wet season. It has an overall appearance closer to a Pacific Northwest rain forest than to a northeast hardwood forest. And it is at 1,500 feet above sea level, just below New Jersey's highest point.

The Kuser Trail is a nature trail with 16 signposts; a descriptive brochure is available at the park headquarters.

Turn left off the main road to the High Point Monument just beyond the end of Lake Marcia. This is a continuation of Kuser Road. In 0.3 mile there is a gate across the road marking the beginning of the Kuser Trail. There is a large parking area at this point as well.

The trail continues on a paved road bed for 0.4 mile where the road bed turns to fine gravel and splits left and right. This is the loop trail around the bog. If you take the left fork, you will skirt the edge of the bog reaching a short (150- foot) side trail connector to the Monument Trail at 1.0 mile from the start of the trail (0.6 mile beyond the fork). The Shawangunk Ridge Trail is co-aligned with the Kuser from this point up to the Monument Trail. The exact location of the trailhead of the Shawangunk Trail is ambiguous since a prominent sign post on this short connector indicates it starts at that point. In reality it is co-aligned with the Kuser and then the Monument Trail and eventually intersects the AT east of the High Point Monument. The Shawangunk Trail blazes become less and less frequent and more and more dim, however, as the AT is approached. So the actual start point, essentially unmarked, is much less obvious to the hiker than the signpost on the short Kuser/Monument Trail connector.

The Kuser Trail is totally inside the loop of the Monument Trail. After crossing an arm of the bog on a broad walk (1.1 to 1.3 miles), a second longer connector leaves to the left, intersecting the Monument Trail near the New Jersey-New York border in 0.35 mile. Continuing on the loop trail, the loop is completed at the fork in 0.25 mile.

Access

There is ample parking at the end of Kuser Road at the trailhead. The Kuser Trail connects to the Monument Trail in two places. Combining the Monument and Kuser trails makes an excellent loop hike.

Trail Surface

The surface is paved for 0.3 mile and fine gravel for 1.4 miles. Boardwalk puncheons cover about 0.2 mile of the trail. In high water conditions some of these may be floating and are not buoyant enough to support a person.

Scenery/Points of Interest

The world's highest eastern bog cedar swamp. It has the appearance of a northern rain forest.

196

Climbing

There are only a couple of minor slopes and a total drop of about 60 feet from the south to the beginning of the swamp loop.

Maintained by: New Jersey Park Service.
Permitted Uses: Hiking only.

The AT & Shawangunk Ridge Trails Beyond the High Point Monument

Shawangunk Ridge Trail   *blue blazed*

The Shawangunk Ridge Trail (SRT) runs north of the High Point Monument to the New Jersey-New York border, eventually joining the Long Path about 35 miles north. In theory, the SRT starts at the AT below the High Point Monument, thus connecting the AT to the Long Path. However, there are no current SRT markings at the AT/Monument Trail intersection where the SRT is supposed to start. There are a few marks where the SRT leaves the Monument Trail and joins the Kuser Trail through the cedar swamp (see page 196).

Thus the SRT at first is co-aligned with the Monument Trail and then the Kuser Trail before heading off north on its own to New York. These co-aligned pieces are discussed elsewhere, so this description is for the SRT from where it leaves the Kuser Trail to the New York border.

The short 150-foot connecting trail joins the Kuser/SRT to the Monument/SRT. There is a prominent signpost at this location indicating the start of the SRT. Turn left onto the Monument Trail at the end of this connector. After running concurrently with the Monument Trail a second time for 200 feet, the SRT turns right. It soon passes a view to the west. At 0.6 mile north of the Monument Trail it turns left and descends on an old woods road to a stream, followed by a gradual rise to the New Jersey-New York border at 1.0 mile from the Monument Trail.

AT Beyond the Monument Trail   *white blazed*

The AT south of its intersection with the Monument Trail is described elsewhere in this section. Beyond the Monument Trail the AT descends the Kittatinny ridge for 1.8 miles and intersects with CO 519 just south of the New Jersey-New York border.

The AT turns right at the cross trail with the Monument Trail, and begins to descend the ridge. At 0.5 mile there is a blue blazed side trail, 0.1 mile long, leading to the High Point Shelter. The trail continues to descend to a small stream at 0.8 mile, turns left and levels out until 1.3 miles, where it turns right and begins to descend on switchbacks. County Route 519 is encountered at 1.8 miles from the Monument Trail. There is parking here for day hikers.

REFERENCE
INFORMATION

- Park Regulations and Facilities
- Hiking Equipment and Etiquette
- Organizations and Emergency Contact Information
- References—Text and Map

Park Regulations and Facilities

Three of the four preserves which cover the Kittatinny range are New Jersey state facilities. A paraphrased list of New Jersey park and forest general regulations follows.

The fourth park is a National Recreation Area administered by the National Park Service, U.S. Department of the Interior.

Appalachian Trail camping regulations are uniform throughout the New Jersey parks and forests. Camping along the AT is generally limited to designated campgrounds or shelters. The AT regulations on federal land are somewhat more liberal.

New Jersey Parks and Forests Pertinent Rules and Regulations from N.J.A.C. 7:2-1 et. seq. (Paraphrased)

A full text of rules is posted and is available upon request.

1.	Alcoholic beverages are prohibited.	7:2-2.6
2.	Furred animals or pets are prohibited from buildings, swimming areas, all camping areas, overnight facilities, golf courses and botanical gardens. Where pets are permitted, they must be held on a six-foot leash.	7:2-2.8
3.	Observe quiet hours 10:00 PM to 6:00 AM.	7:2-2.11
4.	Unduly annoying conduct is prohibited.	7:2-2.11
5.	Dumping of residential, business or commercial waste is prohibited.	7:2-2.7
6.	Waste accumulated from authorized use must be put in provided refuse or recycle containers or taken with the visitor upon departure.	7:2-2.7
7.	Facilities must be occupied and vacated as specified by time and date.	7:2-6.3
8.	Maximum of six (6) people per campsite, lean-to or shelter and six (6) people per yurt, unless all one family.	7:2-6.2
10.	Campsite visitors are allowed from 8 AM to 8 PM (day use fee, if any, required).	7:2-6.6
11.	Maximum fourteen (14) consecutive nights limit for initial stay.	7:2-6.4
12.	Reservations may be canceled. A cancellation fee and the non-refundable reservation fee shall be deducted from any refund due.	7:2-6.8
13.	No refunds to persons evicted.	7:2-6.8
14.	Under-age group campers must have a minimum of one (1) adult supervisor for each nine (9) campers under the age of 18 years.	7:2-6.11
15.	Adult supervisors of under-age group campers must have a vehicle available for emergency transportation.	7:2-6.12

16. The posting of signs, notices, advertisements or any form of solicitation is prohibited.   7:2-2.4

17. No person shall damage, move or remove any plant, animal, equipment, furniture, structure or physical feature of any kind.   7:2-2.10

18. Rules and regulations on posted signs, issued permits and other written or verbal instructions must be followed.   7:2-2.13

19. Where permitted, use of metal detectors requires a permit.   7:2-2.16

20. Possession of firearms is prohibited without specific approval.   7:2-2.17

21. Power boats, sailboats or sail boards may not be operated within 200 feet of a designated bathing area.   7:2-8.6

22. Swimming is restricted to designated areas open and staffed to permit this activity. Diving of any type is prohibited.   7:2-2.20

23. Life jackets must be readily available for every person in a vessel.   7:2-8.13

24. Motor vehicles of all types must be properly registered, licensed and insured.   7:2-3.1

25. Authorized motor vehicles are restricted to established roads and parking areas.   7:2-3.4

26. All-terrain vehicles (ATV's), motorized trail bikes, and off-road vehicles (ORV's) are prohibited.   7:2-3.4

27. Unless otherwise posted, motor vehicle speed is limited to 35 mph on improved roads and 20 mph on dirt, gravel or sand roads.   7:2-3.6

28. Parking of vehicles or related equipment that block traffic on roadways, paths or trails is prohibited.   7:2-3.7

29. Wood fires in campsites are permitted only in fire rings and fireplaces unless fire restrictions are in effect.   7:2-2.12

Source: NJ Department of Environmental Protection, Division of Parks & Forestry, State Park Service

High Point State Park

Road Closures: All park roads southwest of NJ State Route 23 are closed from about the end of firearms hunting season through March. These are Saw Mill Road, Park Ridge Road and the Saw Mill Campground loop road.

Hunting: Hunting is prohibited in the regular hunting season. However, there is a special two-week HPSP deer season when hunting is permitted anywhere in the park. During one of these weeks all hiking is prohibited, including on the AT.

Camping: Camping is permitted at the Saw Mill Campgrounds and the Group Camping Area. On the AT, camping is permitted within sight of Rutherford Shelter or High Point Shelter.

Fires: Open fires are permitted at the campgrounds and picnic area fire grates. No open fires are permitted on the AT.

Cross-Country Skiing: Most of the hiking trails northeast of NJ State Route 23 are managed by a commercial ski concession between December 1 and March 31 when there is sufficient snow cover. Hiking is permitted on the trails, but snowshoes are encouraged.

Boating: Boats without motors or with electric motors are permitted on Lake Marcia and Steeny Kill Lake.

Swimming: Lake Marcia has a small beach which is the only permitted swimming location. Swimming is permitted from Memorial Day to Labor Day. No swimming is allowed at Steeny Kill and Saw Mill lakes.

Interpretive Center: A newly built interpretive center above Lake Marcia's west shore is worth a visit. Extensive displays and an educational program are available.

High Point Monument: The obelisk was designed for internal climbing to the top but the staircase has been closed for many years. In late 2003 it was announced that funds have been made available for repair, and the obelisk will be reopened to the public by late 2004.

Rock Climbing: No significant opportunities exist.

Pets: Permitted on leash except in campgrounds.

Fishing: Licensed fishing is allowed in most locations.

Stokes State Forest

Road Closures: Any time there is snow cover between December 10 and April 15, the following paved roads are closed to traffic:

Dimon Road south of YMCA/Rutgers camp.
Grau Road from Skellinger Road to Crigger Road.
Crigger Road — all.
Sunrise Mountain Road — all except access to AT parking lot at Culvers Gap.

The following unpaved and unmaintained roads are closed anytime there is snow cover and may be closed at other times as well.

Shay Road
DeGroat Road
Brink Road, eastern portion
Skellinger Road (closed to traffic at all times).

Hunting: Allowed on 94% of Stokes State Forest lands. Most of the above mentioned roads are open during hunting season. No hunting is allowed at campgrounds, day use areas, park headquarters, etc.

Swimming: Swimming is allowed only at Stony Lake between Memorial Day and Labor Day.

Camping: On the AT, camping is allowed only at shelters. Camping in the rest of the park is allowed only at four campgrounds: Ocquittunk, Shotwell, Steam Mill and the group campsites.

Fires: No open fires are allowed except at park-provided fireplaces in campgrounds and picnic areas.

Boating: Electric motors or oars or paddles are allowed on lake Ocquittunk only.

Pets: Need to be leashed and are not allowed at overnight facilities.

Cabins: There are 13 cabins for rent in the forest.

Worthington State Forest

Road Closures: None.

Hunting: Permitted in all areas except the river campground.

Camping: On the AT permitted at the backpackers campsite only for multi-day hikers. The river campground is extensive with 69 sites. Reservations are often needed for the river campground, never for the backpackers site.

Fires: Open fires permitted in fire grates at river campground only.

Boating: There is a Delaware River boat launch site at the river campground. No boating on Sunfish Pond.

Swimming: There are no designated beaches in Worthington State Forest. Swimming in Sunfish Pond is not permitted.

Rock Climbing: No significant opportunities within Worthington State Forest.

Pets: Permitted on leash everywhere except river campground.

Fishing: Licensed fishing is allowed in most locations.

Delaware Water Gap National Recreation Area

Road Closures: Blue Mountain Lakes Road and Skyline Drive beyond the Blue Mountain Lakes parking area are closed in winter. Mountain Road (access to Buttermilk Falls) is usually closed in winter. Gravel/dirt portions of Old Mine Road are usually closed in winter.

Hunting: Hunting is allowed in all areas unless marked otherwise. Some private property is posted also. Villages, recreation areas, campsites, education centers and historic districts are all off-limits.

Camping: Allowed only on the AT. In general only multi-day hikers are allowed to camp and in general at least 0.5 mile from the nearest road and 50 to 100 feet from the trail. Camping is also allowed at the AMC Mohican Outdoor Center.

Fires: No open fires are permitted anywhere, except at multi-day river campsites.

Recreation Areas:

Van Campen's Glen	picnicking
Crater Lake	picnicking
Watergate	picnicking
DePue	picnicking, and Delaware River beach
Namanock	picnicking
Kittatinny Point	picnicking, boat launch

Swimming: Encouraged at the DePue lifeguarded beach, but permitted in most locations.

Boating: There are four boat launch sites on the Pennsylvania side of the Delaware River, but only the DePue site on the New Jersey side. All types of water craft are permitted. There are many multi-day traveler campsites along the river. Obtain a river guide brochure from a park visitor center or office. There are fees for boat launching.

Multi-Use Trails: The Slateford Trail has three loops specifically designed for cross-country skiing. Refer to the trail description in the DWG-PA section of this guide.

The Blue Mountain Lakes Trail is available for cross-country skiing and hiking. Bicycling permission is pending and expected to be granted in 2004. This trail is not described in this guide.

Pets: Permitted on leash in all areas except beach, picnic and visitor center areas.

Rock Climbing: Allowed. Rick Rocks (off NPS 602), Mount Tammany and Mount Minsi are all popular areas.

Millbrook Village: A historically preserved 19th century farm village. Obtain an information sheet at the visitors center and park headquarters.

Fishing: Licensed fishing is allowed in all waters unless posted otherwise.

Hiking Equipment and Etiquette

Trail etiquette can be summarized in one brief sentence: *"Do your best to leave behind no evidence that you were there."*

Some of the more prevalent types of evidence which should not be left behind are

1. Litter (if you bring it in, eat it or take it out);
2. Destroyed vegetation off the trail;
3. Wild animals expecting to be fed;
4. Open fire remains.

The etiquette for interaction with other trail users is the same as on a city street.

The trails of the Kittatinny range are ideal for day hiking, including portions of the Appalachian Trail. The AT is also extensively used for multi-day and through hiking. The focus of this guide, however, is the day-hiker. Equipment and supplies recommendations are available for the through-hiker in several AT guides.

The partial list below is aimed at the day-hiker. This list is based solely on the author's experience and may not be all-inclusive and may not cover your specific needs.

Depending on the length of your intended hike, even on a day hike, you can be up to three miles from the nearest road. If the trail is difficult this could be two or three hours of hiking. Therfore, ask yourself what you may need at any time during the day. For a half-day hike or longer, I recommend a small day pack with the following items:

Lunch
Water and/or other drinks (ample)
Maps, guides
Flashlight, compass
Toilet paper
Sun block
Insect repellent
First aid kit
Hat
Hiking stick

Cell phone (service available in most areas)
Dog/leash

Hiking clothing should not be too movement restrictive and needs to be appropriate for the weather conditions, of course. Bad weather of any sort (heat, wind, cold, rain) is likely to be more severe on the trail than in your backyard.

Many hikers prefer maximum skin coverage, long pants and long sleeves, to protect from insects, sun and vegetation.

Shoes need to be comfortable, waterproof, and have stiff heavy soles. The biggest difference between trail walking and street walking is the prevalence of rocks and vegetation which are hard and protrude upward into the soles of your shoes. To stabilize and protect your foot against such things, stiff thick shoes or boot soles are necessary.

On the trail you will sometimes have to walk through mud or water up to a few inches deep requiring waterproof footwear. Many hikers also prefer boots or shoes which cover the ankle as protection against insect bites, scraping rocks and vegetation, or turning your ankle.

Organization Contact Information

Parks and Forests

Worthington State Park
HC 62, Box 2
Columbia, NJ 07832
(908) 841-9575

worth@voicenet.com

High Point State Park
1480 State Route 23
Sussex, NJ 07461
(973) 875-4800

hpsp@warwick.net

Stokes State Forest   stokesst@nac.net
1 Coursen Road
Branchville, NJ 07826
(973) 948-3820

Delaware Water Gap National Recreation Area
New Jersey Office
NJ Ranger Station
2 Walpack-Flatbrookville Road
Layton, NJ 07851
(973) 948-6500

Trail Maintenance & Development Organizations

Appalachian Trail Conference   info@appalachiantrail.org
P.O. Box 807
799 Washington Street
Harpers Ferry, WVA 25425-0807
(304) 535-6331

New York/New Jersey Trail Conference   nynjtc.org
560 Ramapo Valley Road
Mahwah, NJ 07430
(201) 512-9348

Appalachian Mountain Club   amc-ny.org
New York, North Jersey Chapter
5 Tudor City Place
New York, NY 10017
(212) 986-1430

Emergency Phone Numbers

911 or;

New Jersey State Police
(908) 459-5000 (Warren County)
(973) 383-1515 (Sussex County)

Delaware Water Gap National Recreation Area (NJ)
(973) 948-6500

High Point State Park
(973) 875-4800

Worthington State Forest
(908) 841-9575

Stokes State Forest
(973) 948-3820

Warren County, Delaware Water Gap to NPS 602
(908) 835-2000

Sussex County (NPS 602 to High Point)
(908) 579-0875

Selected References *(used in preparation of this book)*

Bertland, D. N., et al. *The Minisink*. Warren County, NJ: Warren County Board of Chosen Freeholders, 1975.

Bull, John, et al. *Birds of North America, Eastern Region*. New York, NY: MacMillan, 1985.

Chazin, Daniel, ed. *New Jersey Walk Book*. 2nd Ed. Mahwah, NJ: New York-New Jersey Trail Conference, 2002.

Kraft, H. C. *The Lenape*. Trenton, NJ: New Jersey Historic Commission, 1986.

National Park Service. *Selected Trails, Delaware Water Gap National Recreation Area*. Washington, DC: U.S. Department of Interior, 2003

New Jersey Department of Environmental Protection. *Cedar Swamp Trail Guide*. Trenton, NJ: Department of Environmental Protection, 2000.

New Jersey Department of Environmental Protection. Park and Forest brochures: High Point State Park, Stokes State Forest, Worthington State Forest, Stokes State Forest Campgrounds. Trenton, NJ: NJ Department of Environmental Protection, 2003.

New York-New Jersey Trail Conference. *Appalachian Trail Guide to New York-New Jersey*. 15th ed. Harpers Ferry, WV: Appalachian Trail Conference, 2002.

Pearce, E. A., et al. *World Weather Guide*. New York, NY: Times Books, 1981.

Pettigrew, L. *New Jersey Wildlife Viewing Guide*. Helena, MT: Falcon Publishing, 1998.

Shaara, Jeff. *The Glorious Cause*. New York, NY: Ballantine Books, 2002.

Sherer, Glen, and Don Hopey. *Exploring the Appalachian Trail: Hikes in the Mid-Atlantic States: Maryland, Pennsylvania, New Jersey, New York*. Mechanicsburg, PA: Stackpole Books, 2001.

Sutton, Ann, and Myron Sutton. *The Appalachian Trail: Wilderness on the Doorstep*. Philadelphia, PA: J. B. Lippincott, 1967.

U.S. Department of Commerce. *Statistical Abstract of the United States*. Washington, DC: U.S. Department of Commerce, 2002.

Warren County Board of Chosen Freeholders. *Historical Sites of Warren County*. Warren County, NJ: Warren County Board of Chosen Freeholders, 1965.

Williams, R., et al. *Over the Mountain: A Place Called Walpack*. Walpack, NJ: Walpack Historical Society, 1988.

Map References

Delorme. *New Jersey Atlas and Gazetteer*. 1st edition, 1999.

Division of Parks & Forestry, State Park Service. *High Point State Park and Stokes State Forest Winter Activities Map*. NJ Department of Environmental Protection, Division of Parks & Forestry, State Park Service.

National Geographic Society. *Historical Atlas of the United States*. Centennial Edition. Washington, DC: National Geographic Society, 2000.

NJ Department of Environmental Protection. *Trail Guide to Stokes State Forest*. Trenton, NJ: NJ Department of Environmental Protection, Division of Parks & Forestry, State Park Service.

NY-NJ Trail Conference. *Kittatinny Trails Map Set**, Nos. 15, 16, 17, 18, 3rd edition, 2000.

Raven Maps. *Pennsylvania and New Jersey*. 1991.

United States Geological Survey*, 7.5' quadrangles: Milford, Port Jervis South, Lake Mashkenozha, Culvers Gap, Branchville, Bushkill, Flatbrookville, Newton West, Stroudsburg, Portland. Washington, DC: United States Department of the Interior, Geological Survey, 1971-1981.

*See key map on next page.

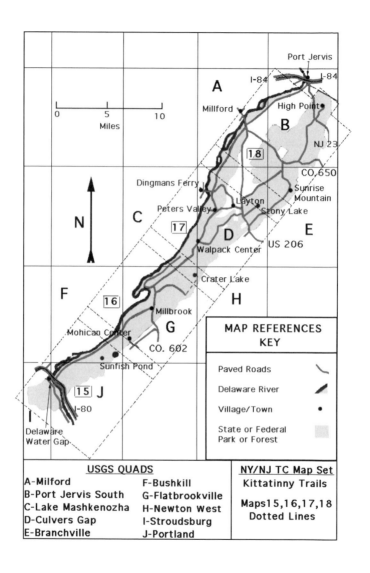

MAP REFERENCES
KEY

Paved Roads

Delaware River

Village/Town

State or Federal
Park or Forest

USGS QUADS

A-Milford
B-Port Jervis South
C-Lake Mashkenozha
D-Culvers Gap
E-Branchville
F-Bushkill
G-Flatbrookville
H-Newton West
I-Stroudsburg
J-Portland

NY/NJ TC Map Set
Kittatinny Trails

Maps15,16,17,18
Dotted Lines

INDEX

Page numbers in **bold** refer to trail descriptions.
Page numbers in *italics* refer to maps.

Emergency phone numbers, 209

Fairview Lake, 88
Farview Parking Area, 42, 44
Farview Trail *See* Beulaland Trail
Flat Brook Road, 143
Flatbrookville, 81
Forked Brook, 161
Fuller Trail, 21, 171, *178*, **183-184**, 185

Gaisler Road, 61, 66
Garvey Springs Trail, 18, 47, *50*, 52, 54, **55-56**, 57
Global Positioning System (GPS), 12, 15
Grau Road, 155, 160, 162, 163, 168
Great Valley of the Appalachians, 1, 27, 41, 64, 66, 71, 73, 86, 92, 158, 176, 188, 190
Gren Anderson Shelter (AT), 152

Hamilton Ridge Trail, 19, *74*, 75, **80-81**, 82
Harding Lake Rock Shelter, 94
Hardwood forest, 6-7, 40, 50, 96, 119, 128, 133, 134, 139, 160, 168, 173, 185, 189, 194, 195
Hemlock Pond, 90, 91, 93
Hemlock Pond Trail, 93
High Point Inn, 5
High Point Monument, 21, 171, 187, 188, 189, 191, 195
High Point Shelter (AT), 198
High Point State Park (HPSP), 2, 5, 9 155, 167, 171, 173, 180
     Monument Trails, **186-198**
          map, *186*

Southwest Trails, 21, **171-185**
     map, *178*
park regulations, 202-203
Hiking equipment and etiquette, 206-207
Holly Springs Trail, 18, 35, *36*, 42, **43-44**, *48*, 49, 50
Horseback riding, 111, 113, 114, 127, 129, 131, 133, 134, 135, 140, 147, 149, 158, 160, 164, 167, 169, 174, 180, 183, 184, 185, 194, 195
Howell Trail, 21, *154*, 155, **158-160**, *166*, 167
Hudson River, 1
Hunting, 111, 113, 114, 127, 129, 131, 133, 134, 135, 140, 147, 149, 160, 164, 167, 169

Iris Trail , 21, 152, 171, *172*, **173-174**, 175, 176, *178*, 179

Jacob's Ladder Trail *See* Ladder Trail
Junco, 46

Kaiser Road Trail, 19, 61, 63, **65-67**, *66*
Karamac Parking Area, 42, 43
Karamac Trail, 18, 35, *36*, **44-45**, 48
Kayser family (Kaiser Road Trail), 65
Kettle holes, 146
Kittatinny Lake, 109, 115, 119
Kittatinny House, 4
Kittatinny Parks, road access, *12*
Kittatinny Range,
     animal species, 7-8
     bird species, 7-8
     description, 1-2
     elevation, 8
     flora and fauna, 6-8

NEW YORK-NEW JERSEY TRAIL CONFERENCE 1920

We invite you to join

the organization of hikers, environmentalists, and volunteers whose tireless efforts produced this edition of *Kittatinny Trails.*

Since our founding in 1920, the **New York-New Jersey Trail Conference's** mission has been to provide the public with the opportunity to directly experience nature and, by doing so, help preserve the region's environmental integrity. The Conference's three-pronged approach— protection, stewardship, and education—is achieved largely through the efforts of volunteers.

Join now and as a member:

■ You will receive the *Trail Walker*, a bi-monthly source of news, information, and events concerning area trails and hiking. The *Trail Walker* lists hikes throughout the New York-New Jersey region by many of our 88 member hiking clubs.

■ You are entitled to purchase our authoritative maps and books at *significant discounts.* Our highly accurate trail maps, printed on durable Tyvek, and our informative guidebooks enable you to hike with assurance in the New York-New Jersey metropolitan region.

■ In addition, you are also entitled to discounts of 10% (and sometimes more!) at most local outdoor stores and many mountain inns and lodges.

■ Most importantly, you will become part of a community of volunteer activists with similar passions and dreams.

Your membership helps give us the clout to protect and maintain more trails. As a member of the **New York-New Jersey Trail Conference**, you will be helping to ensure that public access to nature will continue to expand.

NEW YORK-NEW JERSEY TRAIL CONFERENCE
156 Ramapo Valley Road ❖ Mahwah, NJ 07430 ❖ (201) 512-9348
www.nynjtc.org info@nynjtc.org

Other Hiking Books Available From the Trail Conference!

Authoritative Hiking Maps and Books
by the Volunteers Who Maintain the Trails

CIRCUIT HIKES IN NORTHERN NEW JERSEY

Fifth Edition (2003), Bruce Scofield
Revised and expanded, the author describes 25 hikes
in the NJ Highlands that can be walked without the
need for a car shuttle or significant retracing of steps.
*sc. 176 pgs, 4 3/4 x 6 3/4," B&W photos with maps
for each hike*

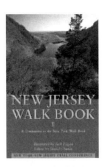

NEW JERSEY WALK BOOK

Second Edition, Edited by Daniel Chazin
Illustrations by Jack Fagan
Essential source book for the New Jersey hiker.
Indispensable reference book, full trail descriptions,
illustrations, color maps, ecology, geology, and history.
Companion to the *New York Walk Book.*
sc. 442 pgs, 53/8 x 81/8, B&W illus.

DAY WALKER:
32 hikes in the New York Metro Area

Second Edition (2002)
A collection of 32 walks in the New York metropolitan
area for new and experienced hikers. The *Day Walker*
presents a sample of walks within 60 miles of the
George Washington Bridge, of varying levels of
difficulty and most accessible by public transport.
sc. 301 pgs, 53/8 x 8 1/8, B&W photos and maps.